RINGS, SWINGS & CLIMBING THINGS

RINGS, SWINGS & CLIMBING THINGS

RITA HOPPERT, ED. D.

CONTEMPORARY
BOOKS, INC.
CHICAGO

Library of Congress Cataloging in Publication Data

Hoppert, Rita.
 Rings, swings, and climbing things.

 Includes index.
 1. Wooden toy making. 2. Muscle strength.
3. Motor ability in children. I. Title.
TT174.5.W6H66 1985 688.7 85-13964
ISBN 0-8092-5264-3

Published by Contemporary Books, Inc.
180 North Michigan Avenue, Chicago, Illinois 60601
Manufactured in the United States of America
Library of Congress Catalog Card Number: 85-13964
International Standard Book Number: 0-8092-5264-3

Published simultaneously in Canada by Beaverbooks, Ltd.
195 Allstate Parkway, Valleywood Business Park
Markham, Ontario L3R 4T8 Canada

This book is dedicated to Bruce.

CONTENTS

ACKNOWLEDGMENTS

Five years flew by between the start of this project and the publication of the book. In that time, many people helped me toward its completion.

First, I must thank Joe Cockerill for his invaluable advice, training, and support in photography. Without the pictures this book would not be the practical guide that it is, and Joe helped me to learn to see through a lens. He and his wife, Vicki, conceptualized and took the cover shots.

I also want to thank the mothers and fathers who opened their homes to my work:

Sally and Charlie Moomaw
Pam and Mike Runyan
Sandy and Bill McCusker
Teresa and Mike Pachan
Jan and John Anderson
Patty and Leo Buse, Jr.
Sue and Steve Mueller
Gwen Agna and Tom Marantz
Debby and Pete Cassinelli
Roma and Chris Albers
Mindy and Jim Thomas
Mary and Ed Neill
Sadie and Leo Buse
Marilyn and Ardy Wander

And to the children, parents, and grandparents who played on the equipment and patiently posed for the photography:

Bruce, Roma, and Heinz Hoppert
Pam, Mike, Christopher, Emily, and Cameron Runyan
Debby, Ann, Peter, and Elizabeth Cassinelli
Mary, Louisa Jane, and Foster Joseph Neill
Sally, Peter, and Jeffery Moomaw
Gwen and Nel Agna
Sandy and Sarah McCusker
Roma, Emily, and Katherine Albers
Mindy, Christy, and Hiller Thomas
John and Travis Anderson
Patty, Lee, and Leslie Buse
Nancy, Joseph, and Melany DeMarco
Lauren Morah Ahrens
Shelley Ingbers
Adam Wander
Michelle Whitney
Teresa and Annie Pachan
Sadie and Leo Buse
Dana and Keven Matsuzaka
Brian Gist
Mrs. J. A. Neill
Scott Schuh
Emma Carlson-Berne
Daryl Elliott

A thank you is given to the personnel at Robin Color Lab for their professional work, to the women who typed different parts of the manuscript, and to Sally and Bruce, who did some timely editing. I also want to thank Richard Boyer, Jr., for professionally redrawing my diagrams.

Contemporary Books agreed to publish this book, and I am forever grateful. David Stuart handled the project, and I thank him for his enthusiasm and work. I would also like to thank Amy Teschner and Robb Pawlak.

Some people who prepared me for the title of author also deserve credit. Thank you to Drs. June Sciarra and Dan Wheeler for all the work on my dissertation, which is now bearing a different fruit, and to the late Hilda Rothschild for her emotional support to a student and friend.

Thanks to my sitters, Barb Schmitt and Erica Whitney, who gave me the peace of mind to concentrate on the book.

The people that receive the deepest thanks are my family, Bruce, Roma, and Heinz.

RINGS, SWINGS & CLIMBING THINGS

PLANNING CHILD-CENTERED SPACES

1
GETTING STARTED

Rings, Swings, and Climbing Things is a combination how-to manual and child development book designed to help parents and other child-centered adults help children play and learn. The projects are for large-muscle equipment, a term borrowed from early childhood education jargon. It means any equipment that can be used to stimulate the muscles that control locomotion or the unrefined movements of the arms and upper body. (Large or gross motor movement is different from fine motor movement, which is control of the muscles of the hands and fingers, the feet and the mouth, requiring tight eye-hand coordination.)

The benefits of supplying children with this type of equipment can go beyond muscle stimulation. Indeed, both children and parents can receive many benefits from applying some basic developmental principles to children's play, using the equipment in this book as a tool for learning and playing.

STORY OF THE BOOK'S DEVELOPMENT

There is nothing like this book on the market. I feel justified in making that statement because I painstakingly researched the materials on child-centered spaces available in bookstores and libraries while working on my doctoral thesis. I had the experience of designing, implementing, and then evaluating a home-based Head Start program (a federally funded preschool program). Part of the project involved parent education, and I planned and delivered a series of workshops on child-centered spaces in the home. Presenting to young and struggling parents the materials that I had found was embarrassing for me. The examples were such slick and expensive settings, cute but nonfunctional spaces, and difficult carpentry projects that the parents were immediately frustrated. The child development books were no help either; they contained theories but no practical applications (and no pictures). The authors of the available material were interior designers, architects, carpenters, and child development researchers.

I decided to design my own projects, to come up with my own ideas. The need for a book like this would be obvious to parents: Large muscle activity *indoors* drives most parents crazy, mainly because houses and apartments lack space and equipment to channel effectively children's everpresent energy. The equipment available for the school market is expensive and is not readily available to parents. What is available in toy stores is geared to the toddler, is plastic, and is "over-smurfed."

Since there was little appropriate large-muscle equipment on the commercial market, and current books were very little help, and many parents seemed to have limited financial resources to solve this problem, the need for a how-to book about make-it-yourself large-muscle equipment was obvious.

Finishing my degree, I began conceptualizing this book. It was to be my "employment" since I would be home for a while with our second child. My husband, Bruce, and I had a daughter, Roma, who was two and a half at the time her brother was born. In fact, he was delivered the day before graduation ceremonies in June 1980. Allowing for recovery, I started my own "home-based" program seven weeks later.

In late July, I invited a group of six friends to meet each week to work on projects for our children. I focused on large-muscle equipment that was inexpensive and on homemade alternatives to expensive, store-bought playthings. We met for 18 months, building the projects that I designed and trying them in our homes. During that year and a half we discussed our needs and the needs of our children and produced some designs that helped both parents and children.

At our first meeting, my six friends agreed that there was a need for large muscle equipment *indoors*. We discussed solutions to our problems that matched both child and family needs. My master's degree and classroom experience in Montessori Education provided the philosophical underpinnings for the solutions, and my full-day child-care experience provided the practical approaches to the problems. The women that I worked with deserve a great deal of credit for their contributions to the book as well as for their construction of the projects. Besides being parents, they each brought special talents to the group. Roma Albers, mother of one, made graphic design items for local shops. Gwen Agna, mother of a daughter, taught nursery school. Debby Cassinelli was the full-time mom of three, including twins, at the time we started the book. Sally Moomaw, mother of two boys, worked as a nursery school teacher and is the author of the book *Discovering Music in Early Childhood* (Allyn and Bacon, 1984). Sandy McCusker was a former nursery schoolteacher and the mother of one. Pam Runyan taught piano to young children and was the mother of three children. Pam, Sandy, and Gwen have each had another child; Debby and Roma have each had two children since we ended our weekly meetings.

Please do not think I am slighting the fathers by not mentioning them in these credits. A few were involved at various times, but for the most part it was the women who built the equipment in our original group.

I have always credited my mother with teaching me how to use tools that now she cannot remember ever using. At least she taught me how to wing it successfully without formal training in carpentry. My husband, who is an engineer by discipline, taught me the finer points of tool use and also rechecked all my plans for their design characteristics.

It's interesting to note here that this book focuses on what is traditionally a mother's domain, the home and children, combined with what is traditionally a father's domain, the workshop. Whether you are a mother or a father, or a child-oriented individual of either sex, I hope that those of you who feel intimidated by tools will find this book a stepping stone to mastering a new skill. You should find the photos in this book especially helpful—and reassuring. Except for the construction pictures, which are close-ups of the projects, the photos show children, not models, using the projects in a variety of ways and in a variety of settings. The photos also support the premise of this book, that children are active learners, and the gleeful expressions on the children's faces should convince you that this equipment truly serves its purpose.

The pictures were taken in the homes of the people who made the projects. Some of the settings might look large, but believe me, they were not. For purposes of clarity in the photography, I did some temporary shifting of furniture to get an uncluttered shot of the project. Also, some of the pictures were taken with a wide angle lens that seems to open up spaces and make them appear larger than they really are. These homes and apartments are in Cincinnati, Ohio; your weather, topography, and flora will differ, but the play of children is the same.

Because I was teaching part-time at two local universities, the writing and photography took about three years. Therefore, you will see some of the children as toddlers, and, a few pages later, as preschoolers. The book finished, I began writing to publishers. The breakthrough came in October 1984, when Contemporary Books called to tell me after four years of work that my book was finally to be a reality!

WHAT'S IN THIS BOOK

Rings, Swings, and Climbing Things is divided into three sections. Part I continues setting the stage for the projects with a discussion of children as active learners, some tips for planning indoor large-muscle activities, and some considerations concerning who will get involved in your projects.

Part II tells you all about the materials and tools you'll need, where to buy them, and how to use them. To show how easy it is to get involved in building equipment for children, Part II ends with a sample easy-to-build project and instructions for making a woodworking bench. Those of you who are familiar with carpentry may be able to skip this section, or just use it as a handy reference, and move on to the projects you want to try.

Part III gives easy-to-read instructions for building more than 30 large-muscle projects, complete with photos for each. This section concludes with pointers on moving the indoor equipment outdoors for those who have yards, porches, and other outdoor spaces suitable for children's play.

2
CHILDREN ARE
ACTIVE LEARNERS

Why prepare a home environment for children's play, especially their large-muscle play? The major reason is that play should be respected for the many things children learn through it. *Play* is a misleading word in our culture. Children are constantly mastering the world. That is, they are learning every minute the way things work, the way their bodies work, and the way people get along (or don't get along). Whether they are examining different raisins in their bread, taking two stairs at a time, or pretending to be a mommy or a daddy, their play is their work of discovery and personal development. This work deserves the greatest respect.

Children are active learners; *active* means not only that movement is a component of learning, but also that children are organizers of their own perceptions. They are not the "blank slates" that they were once thought to be. They actively fit knowledge into their previous frameworks of viewing the world, either adding it to old information or changing that old information to fit all the new facts. For example, a toddler who slides for the first time can log this experience as movement without moving arms or legs (moving arms or legs is old information learned through crawling and walking) and as movement without force by another person (the new aspect is gravity).

Children generally are active in learning. They manipulate the environment, including both things and people. They experiment with things and with the roles that people play in relation to the children themselves. Sometimes the manipulation is not observable. With the beginning of preoperational thought, at around age two, children can manipulate in their heads before they start moving things around with their hands. Prior to about age two, children have one way of conceptualizing, and that is through sensorimotor knowledge. They know through and by storing information in terms of sensations and movement. For

example, a child sees Dad hang the baby swing and knows it by seeing its position in space and by "feeling" the rocking motion before it even starts. Adults still think in a sensorimotor mode when they "experience" riding on a Ferris wheel while only thinking about it; that is sensorimotor knowledge.

After age two, children can think in terms of pictures as well. Later, they add thinking in terms of language concepts. The ability to move around, combine, and

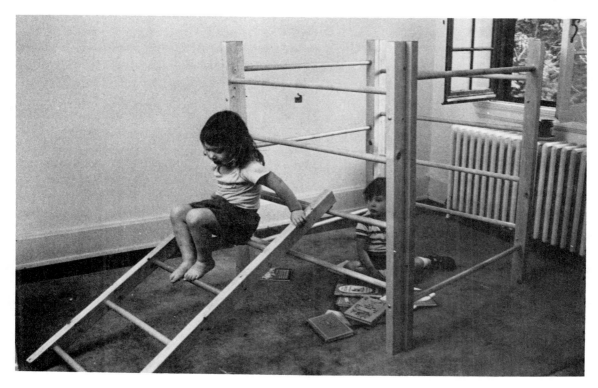

change thoughts in the forms of sensorimotor, pictorial, or language concepts allows children to understand things much more quickly than when they can only learn through action, as is the plight of children in their first year.

Play is the same work of mastering the environment. Children depend on two principles when deciding to act: novelty and repetition. Children are drawn to anything that is new enough to their experience to excite curiosity but also familiar enough that they can approach it with some idea of the nature of the thing. In other words, there must be enough novelty to attract them but also some past experience to give them guidance.

Repetition is important in play to confirm hypotheses and allow for experimentation. Practicing a skill over and over refines sensorimotor knowledge.

A developmental philosophy is based on the principle that children learn certain things in sequences, building one skill on another. When certain foundations are laid, other skills can be mastered. Observant adults can provide experience in foundational "blocks of knowledge or skill," and children can build these into repertoires of behavior that make multiskill demands on them. Thus, a child who can catch, understand a my turn/your turn relationship, and pay attention for a period of time can play toss with her brother.

Parents who appreciate the amount of energy and repetition necessary for children to attain a skill, whether motor, cognitive, or social, and who appreciate the role of an environment that encourages exploration and practice, help children reach their potential.

The adult's role in play is not only passive, preparing the environment; it is active as well. Parents are the primary teachers of their children. They are the first teachers and, with the love bond, the most salient teachers. *Teacher* is used in a loose sense here and does not imply that adults should organize and direct play. Modeling is the most effective way of teaching. Adults play with children and model cooperativeness, graciousness, patience. Children learn leader/follower behavior, turn-taking behavior, etc., by seeing it and practicing it in play. Dad and daughter, sending a toy truck down a ramp over and over, say, "Your turn," "May I please try it?" and "I would like to be after you." (Daughter does not even have to be verbal to say these things.)

Through positive language and success-inspiring activities, Mom and Dad can build in the children good self-images. The children feel their worth and their ability to succeed. When parents respond to their success in doing a chore with a comment like "That was a good job," the words reflect on the action; saying "You're a good boy," on the other hand, puts their personal goodness or badness at stake. The work, not the child's conscience, should always be the focus of the comment.

Because children bring a strong sense of autonomy to the play situation, adults might not always be welcome as participants. When adults courteously and respectfully apologize for intruding, they are worthy models. Yes, it is hard to be rejected by a two-year-old! But when adults take the children's point of view, they can see that this is not personal rejection but the statement "I need to do it myself."

Children also bring their own temperaments to bear on the play situation. Observant parents know when children are in the mood for play, about how long it should last, and when too much stimulation or change is upsetting them. They know when children want to be wrestled and when they want to be read to.

Sometimes it is hard for adults to separate their egos and their needs from those of their children. It becomes a contest of egos. It is best to avoid this power struggle because the only way adults usually can win is to use bribery or physical force. Neither is a good alternative. Children have the goal, will, attention span, and natural drive to do it themselves, and this puts adults at a disadvantage.

Now that the social, emotional, and cognitive aspects of play have been discussed, we can speak to the physical aspects of play. Active children, active in play that is appropriate, safe, and engrossing, are people who will grow and develop in your care.

3
PLANNING FOR LARGE-MUSCLE ACTIVITY INDOORS

Five factors must be considered when planning for activity inside: space, storage, discipline, children's abilities, and your personal tolerances.

SPACE

Large-muscle activity means movement, and movement requires some space. In the smaller quarters of young families, the space does not have to be a permanent one, reserved for only one purpose.

The first step in finding space is determining where the children play, underfoot or off on their own.

The second step is to take stock of the house or apartment. Which rooms are used often (like the kitchen), and which rooms are used only for specialized or short-term activities? In many homes the dining room is often used only for dinner; the bedroom might be used only for sleeping. Why not push the dining room table up against the wall for the better portion of the day and use its space? Why not combine two children's bedrooms making one a sleeping room and the other a playroom? Why not rearrange the living room to include a child-centered part and an adult part? Creative thinking about rooms that had labels defining their activity might be all that you need to do to come up with a way to share adult-centered homes with young children.

A space as small as five feet by six feet can house a shelf of toys and books, one small mat, and a climber (either out or folded next to the shelf), and the door near it can house the doorway gym.

STORAGE

When children have finished playing, they put away their activities; they learn to respect their toys and space just as you do. If the respect does not come

naturally, then the toys can be put away *out of sight*. (This will be discussed later.)

A low set of shelves, with about eight to ten spots for toys, displays playthings in an orderly and untangled manner. Families with more than one child can double the shelf space to allow for a variety of interests in toys. Even with three or four children in a family, there is overlap in the kinds of toys played with, so there is no need to multiply toy space radically. Shelves make the toys both easy to put away and easy to retrieve for play. With only eight or so choices to scan visually to make a choice of playthings, the children are not overwhelmed by sheer quantity.

Children experience a sense of order (not to be confused with neatness) in their late toddler, early preschool years that helps them understand cause/effect, sequential ordering, and purposefulness. The shelves aid in organizing their space, which in turn improves their mental organization.

With only eight or so toys in the playroom, living room, or bedroom, where are

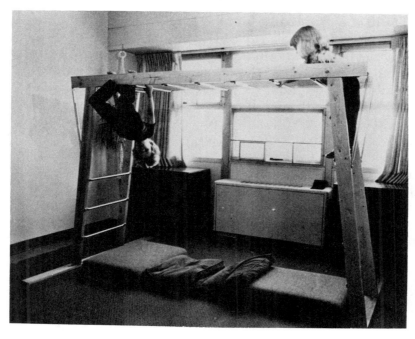

the other mountains of toys that children seem to end up with? They are tucked away on the upper shelf of a closet, stacked on a shelf in the garage or basement, or boxed in the apartment's storage locker. Have trade-in days every three to five weeks with stored-away items for a whole new shelf of toys; children will enjoy playing with things that have not been out for awhile. Tell the children that the storage place is off-limits; as they realize the function of the trade-in shelf, they will come to appreciate the storehouse. Trade-in offers novelty because the children, with an older point of view the next time a toy is on display, approach them in a way different from before. Trade-in offers repetition because they can play with the toys in a more mature way six times over a two-year period. The toy exchange is great when Mom or Dad has to get some work done without interruption; fifteen minutes for putting out new materials will keep the children working for two hours. Putting away some toys and limiting what the children have access to aids in keeping their play space neat and the toy's pieces together, as it is easier to keep a limited number of toys organized.

DISCIPLINE

Because the equipment presented in this book is storable (except for box climbers), it can be removed when the children are not using it according to family rules. The best time to establish a routine is the first day that each project is introduced. The rules should cover toy use from storage place to play and back to storage place. When the precedent is set on the first day, and is established for all the toys, the rules are easy to remember because they are the same for all the activities. It is the children's responsibility to follow the rules and it is your responsibility to make them.

It all sounds so easy, but there will be times when the play space will look like a toy store hit by an earthquake. The rules you set will make even general cleanup easier for the children as they will not have an overwhelming amount of equipment to put away.

When the rules are not followed and they result in small accidents, you can make such incidents lessons in natural consequences. It does not take a long lecture to point out the problem. A simple statement like "If you hold on with two hands, you might not fall backward," suffices. Lectures involve the emotions and cloud the simple message that you are trying to get across. All the statement has to include is what happened and the consequence. No judgments!

Big accidents demand an analysis of the situation. Is the child strong enough? Is the space too small? Is the equipment in good repair? Is the space suffering from the demands of too many children? Posing and answering such questions will give you an idea of how to act on the problem.

When the problem is sharing (discussed in depth in the introduction to Chapter 10), the adult usually gets involved in settling the dispute. Sometimes, with a little more time than parents are willing to give, the children can settle the problem themselves. When the problem degenerates into hurting, the adults can step in, separate the battlers, and offer to hold the plaything until the children solve their problem. If they cannot solve it, then the adult might offer a number of solutions from which they can choose. The idea is that the adults should *not* step in as judge and jury; the adults then become third parties in a problem that is not theirs. It belongs to the children, and they, with time and sometimes suggestions, can settle it. Then the problem *and* the solution are theirs.

With toddlers, the rules for sharing do not work. They are egocentric by nature.

In arguments between two of them, distraction is the best solution. One usually gets tired of the problem and eliminates himself. When the adult does have to step in, offering another activity usually works.

An altercation between a toddler and an older child is a different kind of problem. It is important to protect the rights of the older child to play. The toddler, with a shorter attention span and infinite curiosity, wants to see what big brother or sister is up to. One solution is that the older child can be taught how to show the toddler the work and wait out the younger child's attention span. Another solution is, again, distracting the toddler; some siblings become masters at this ploy. Sometimes the only solution is to remove the toddler and give big sister or brother his or her space. It helps to remember that toddlers will not always be toddlers.

A language tool that is very effective when it becomes part of a family's vocabulary is to say, "This is my work," or "This is her work." It reinforces the concept that all children (and adults) have the right to their chosen activities. Since play is so important to cultivate, it should not be interrupted arbitrarily by anyone. That includes parents!

CHILDREN'S ABILITIES

Sometimes it is hard to separate adult fantasies from children's reality. Even though you may want to make all the projects in this book, they might not all fit into your environment. Be selective and critical about what could be overstimulating or developmentally inappropriate for your children.

Introducing an activity too early, one that a child cannot master, might cause frustration or accidents. The piece of equipment can be put away quietly and brought out in two or three months for another try. *When introducing the doorway gym equipment or climber for the first time, always put the exercise mat under it to protect the children.*

Younger siblings will try out older siblings' equipment. They will not normally be frustrated by such attempts because they at least have a model for the equipment's use, and they know that one day they will be as big and as skilled as their older brothers or sisters. But they will need that safety cushion underneath.

PERSONAL TOLERANCES

Some days large-muscle activity will drive you crazy. For those times, try putting on some slow, soft music to counteract your mood and hopefully slow down the children. Some days the children will seem frustrated; getting them involved in gross motor movement may bring some relief. Or the opposite may work; change the large-muscle work to fantasy play with a blanket over the climber.

Most of the time, with the prepared environment, large-muscle activity will be an accepted part of the household routine. Positive action will solicit positive attention. Children will ask for your attention to a new trick rather than to their jumping on the couch. When something negative does happen, you can counter with a positive suggestion like "The exercise mat was made for jumping." Using positive language, focusing on concrete solutions, is a great mood enhancer and reduces the need for discipline, which is not a mood enhancer.

When your tolerance is low and you seem to be getting on each other's nerves, try novelty! Find something totally new to add to the child's life. Be creative. Share your unbreakable kitchen utensils, make a new project together, rearrange adult and child space, add music to walking the walking boards, have a trade-in day, suggest a new theme around which to pretend, and even supply a few props. Even a child can be bored occasionally.

4
THE ROLE OF ADULTS

WORKING ALONE OR DEVELOPING A TOY GROUP

Both of these systems have advantages. Forming a toy group gives novice carpenters the support of other group members, but even when working alone, a great amount of help can be found. Lumberyard workers, hardware store personnel, spouses, relatives, and friends can give advice when it is needed.

Working alone, you can create a project in those snatches of time between naps and preparing meals or after work but before a favorite TV program. If you have a basement, a garage, or another space, then the project can sit until a little time is worked free. All the big projects can be made in a weekend and the little ones in a matter of hours. Working alone also affords the luxury of working with or parallel to your children. When a step in the project comes up that the children can complete, they make an investment in their own toys and get the satisfaction of mastering a new skill. And you have the satisfaction of being their teacher.

When you already have all the tools and necessary skills for projects, working alone should pose no problem. It may be a little more expensive to buy the wood and hardware that is sold in quantity only on your own, but you can store the extras and use them for future projects.

If you lack all or some of the tools and skills and the space to work, then forming a cooperative of friends is a good approach. One person can supply a drill, another the space, a third, some carpentry experience, and so on. In a group, support can be social as well as physical; discussing the latest in temper-tantrum solutions or the newest movies is done as easily over a saw as it is over cards.

Working in a group also allows you to buy lumber and hardware in quantity. Eyelets, screws, springs, etc., are sold in bulk packages. Wood is sold in sheets or

15

in a minimum number of feet. Although scraps left from one project can often be used in another, the less the waste, the lower the cost.

Working in groups is also an advantage in that making a commitment to meet regularly transforms the projects from ideas on paper to reality.

NOTES FOR CHILD-CENTERED ADULTS

To Parents

This book was written primarily for moms and dads and children. It was written for renters and owners; it was written for those who live in small places and not so small places. It was written for those who move often and those who are not so mobile. In the story of the different climbers and their owners, I hope you see a little of your own family.

To Grandparents

Sometimes you entertain your grandchildren in your home. It might help your peace of mind to provide them a space that is theirs in a home that is not as child-centered as it used to be when their parents were young. Or you might try a project as a holiday or birthday gift, something Grandpa made himself!

To Daycare Home Providers

You are an ever-growing group of people who care for children. I hope that when you read *parent* in this book you will consider yourself addressed as well, since you are the primary caretakers for a long stretch of the day—or night.

Active children, active in play that is appropriate, safe, and engrossing, are people who will grow and develop in your care. Find time to make the projects by involving them in construction. Involve them in laying the ground rules and in choosing a storage place for these materials in which you all have an investment.

To Teachers

I have conducted many workshops on the projects in this book for the parent groups of infant/toddler and preschool programs. Some have been held to introduce the concepts of creating equipment to meet children's natural needs; others have been actual work sessions in which we made selected projects. In all cases the parents loved them; the workshops gave them concrete ideas about working with their children or something concrete to work on with their children. I encourage you to try to develop a parent night or series of parent nights from the material in this book.

While the parents are busy making projects, you and they can be discussing discipline approaches or cognitive development; instead of lecturing, the ideas are imbedded in practical and concrete play ideas. Parents appreciate both the approach and the work that they can take pride in doing. It is good public relations for you and your school to have a successful and involved parent group.

If you decide to make some of the projects for school use, I caution you to remember that they were designed for home use, where the wear and tear is much less. The materials will not hold up quite as long as they would when used by only one or two children for part of the day.

To Child Care Professionals

As a professional, I know that there are many ways that you could utilize the information in this book. For parent and family counselors, for trainers of home care providers and intervention workers, for teacher trainers and infant/toddler stimulation trainers, I wrote this material and hope that your trainees enjoy it.

TO ALL READERS

Whatever category you fall into, I would be interested in hearing your comments about your experiences with the projects and ideas presented in this book. Please write to me in care of *Contemporary Books, 180 North Michigan Avenue, Chicago, IL 60601.*

II

MATERIALS AND CONSTRUCTION

5
MATERIALS

LUMBER SUPPLIERS

There are two breeds of lumber dealers: the self-serve store and the lumber-yard. The latter almost always has the stock that you want in the length that you want to buy. The self-serve lumber stores have their stock displayed in standard lengths, usually 4', 8', and 12'. The lumber that you want might not always be in stock, but it is usually cheaper than at lumberyards.

Lumberyards have a huge quantity of stock because they are in the business of supplying builders. They carry many grades of lumber, from rough construction grades to smooth, knot-free timber in a variety of woods like pine, redwood, fir, and hardwoods. In order to get the wood, buyers usually go to a desk and place an order for the quantity, quality, and length desired; that means that buyers must know what they want beforehand. After the order is placed and paid for, the wood is picked up from a stockperson.

To get the most help and personal attention, first shop around for a yard. Second, it is best to go to the yard between 10:00 and 12:00 or 1:30 and 3:00. A large yard generally serves its builder customers first thing in the morning and last thing in the afternoon; the personnel will tend to be more helpful when not rushed. Lumberyards usually have a small, stable staff that is easy to get to know. Third, get to know the people who pick out and load up purchases. Let them know that you are building something for children and need a straight, unwarped piece. Usually they will be most accommodating. Last, take along this book for a visual aid if a question arises that you do not know how to answer.

A service that most lumberyards provide is that of cutting pieces to special lengths. Sometimes they charge a sawing fee, and other times they will cut it for free just so it will fit into a car. Inquire as to the servies available. When buying plywood, having it precut to specific dimensions is a real bonus!

Shopping at self-serve lumber stores calls for a different procedure. First, all the wood is displayed; therefore, the pieces are self-selected. Warped, split, or poor-quality lumber is easy to avoid, and smaller pieces of sheet wood like Masonite and plywood are available in 2×2 and 4×4 sizes. Second, buyers must know what they are looking for because wood of different qualities and grades comes with a variety of different names. Third, the personnel may or may not be helpful or available; some stores pride themselves on their salespeople, while others hire stock people who are not necessarily handy. Fourth, lumber stores usually have other departments—namely, hardware, paint, and tools—that make one-stop shopping easy.

A few stores have departments that will cut your wood to specific dimensions; check out the outlets in the area for this valuable service.

Some lumberyards and stores have mills attached. Mills are highly specialized shops that can fabricate anything in wood. Usually they are called upon by builders for custom windows and the like. They can prepare your wood, including drilling and sanding, to your exact specs—all you do is assemble the pieces. Of course this is all done for a fee, but for some people it might be worth checking out.

Another thing to check out is the scrap pile of wood from a mill or lumberyard. Often they throw away exactly the piece that would make a good base for the ring toss or another project. If you cannot use the wood, the children will enjoy working with you, using these scraps as their own lumber. This is another good reason to befriend the yard workers!

Lumber

As in all industries, lumber has its own jargon to refer to different types and qualities of wood. All the woods that are called for in the projects are described in each project, starting with three kinds of sheet wood: plywood, particleboard, and Masonite.

Plywood is made of thin layers of wood glued on top of each other, pressed and dried. It comes in a number of thicknesses, starting at ¼", and normally is sold in 4'×8' sheets. It also comes in a number of grades (qualities). Interior grade has one smooth surface with no knots and one rough side. Exterior grade plywood has one side that may have repaired knots or splits and one rough side.

Particleboard is a manufactured wood made from sawdust and glue. It is very hard and heavy. Masonite is another manufactured wood. It is made with wood fiber and resin and can be made in very thin sheets. Both are inappropriate for use in long spans as they crack easily when overstressed.

Framing lumber includes 1×2s, 2×2s, 2×3s, and 2×4s. The funny thing about a 2×4 is that its dimensions are not exactly 2" × 4". Pine shelving board is also misnamed in relation to size. The folowing table gives the actual measurements.

Nominal Stock Dimension	Actual Size (in inches)
1 × 1	⅝ × ⅝
1 × 2	⅝ × 1⅝
1 × 3	⅝ × 2⅝
1 × 4	⅝ × 3⅝
1 × 6	⅝ × 5½
1 × 8	⅝ × 7½
1 × 10	⅝ × 9¼
1 × 12	⅝ × 11¼
2 × 2	1½ × 1½
2 × 3	1½ × 2½
2 × 4	1½ × 3½

The grades of the above woods range from construction grade to wood totally free of knots. Construction grade wood is generally rough pine with knots in it; sometimes it is bowed, warped, or cracked. Even within one grade of wood, quality can vary. With careful scrutiny, even construction grade wood can yield a good piece of timber. To check for straightness, lay it on the ground and roll it; all four sides should touch the ground along the whole length of board. Ask for the "best" piece at the lumberyard or pick it out yourself at the do-it-yourself stores. Construction grade wood is the least expensive and, with some good sanding, is fine for most of the projects.

For each kind of board, there are different names for different grades. No. 2 pine and clear fir are just two grades that would require less sanding work but at a big jump in price.

Pine is a softwood; it is less dense than hardwoods and therefore is lighter and easier to cut. Fir is a kind of evergreen related to pine; it is a softwood but is a little harder to drill and cut than pine. Redwood is another type of softwood that is easy to work with, lightweight yet strong. Hardwoods like maple, oak, and birch are costly, weightier, and difficult to work with using hand tools.

Dowels are made from both hardwood and softwood. The ones that are usually sold in hardware stores are pine and are by far the easier with which to work; lumberyards carry them in denser hardwoods as well.

Baseboard woods like lattice and trim boards come in a variety of shapes; they are knotfree, are milled in decorative faces, and presanded until smooth.

Wood is a natural material that is not made under a quality-control program. *Its strength varies in relation to the grain and to its internal structure.* When working with wood, you'll discover that no two pieces are alike. For example, baseball bats that look solid can crack on contact with a ball. Befriend the people at your lumber supply store; explain your wood needs, and they will help you choose the best pieces.

HARDWARE STORES

For me, hardware stores are often the birthplace of ideas. Walking up and down the aisles, I might see an item and think that it would be perfect to solve a problem, or it might inspire a use totally different from the one for which it was intended.

The best hardware stores are the locally owned ones with an owner who knows everything in stock. You can often present the owner with a problem and get the solution in a very unorthodox way. Some proprietors are more pleasant than others, but they are all knowledgeable. The stores carry a ton of stock crammed into every corner of the space; that is usually why it is best to have a guide. Some locals even carry a small amount of lumber, such as 2×2s, 2×3s, and 2×4s. They also carry dowels, rope, and aluminum pipe. Their hardware and tool sections are likely to have all that is called for in this book. The one drawback is that the prices are higher than at the big discount hardware stores, but you have to pay for neighborhood service and knowledge!

The large hardware stores cannot match the small stores for service, although the personnel may have some knowledge of their departments. It is best to shop in the large discount stores for specific items that are needed in quantity like rope, screws, and dowels, or for costly items like casters and polyurethane, to get the best price. These large stores are also the place to browse the wide-open aisles for ideas. Have a shopping list of specific items that you need whenever you go to a hardware store; it is tremendously frustrating to have some time to work on a project and find that you do not have a piece of hardware or the right number of screws.

6
CONSTRUCTION TIPS

This section details the tools required to build the projects in this book and gives some helpful hints on the optimum way to use the tools. Novice carpenters will find it helpful to read over the helpful hints before trying a new skill so that the wood is not wasted through unnecessary mistakes. Always practice something new once or twice on scrap wood; it takes only ten seconds to practice drilling a hole.

Part of the theme of this book is that parents and child-centered adults find satisfaction in making equipment for their children. If this includes becoming competent in tool skills, so much the better. Becoming competent also includes learning *when to ask for help*. Friends who are knowledgeable about tools are great to tap for advice, suggestions, and demonstrations of skills that you learn best by example. The next-best people to ask for advice are the people at your neighborhood hardware store. They are in the business of supplying you with your hardware needs. Take full advantage of their expertise.

Basic tools are required for the projects; some of them are found in those kitchen drawer toolboxes. Others might need to be bought. The best suggestion when purchasing tools is to buy a quality tool, taking into consideration budget and amount of expected use. Good tools, taken care of (not left exposed to weather), last a long time. There are also ways to avoid purchasing tools, like having wood precut and sharing them in a toy group.

MEASURING AND SQUARING

Not all yardsticks are created equal. There can be as much as ¼" variation among average wooden sticks. Measuring tapes are more accurate. When marking spots or drawing lines, use a sharp pencil or even a ballpoint pen for a clear and precise measure. When measuring the same distance a number of times in succession, mark right on the yardstick or tape the inch mark and then reposition for the next mark; you will get the same measure each time. Be careful to measure all matching pieces from the same ends, as when building a ladder.

Measuring a line for sawing requires special accuracy. There is a tool called a *straightedge* that you line up with the edge of the wood to draw a perpendicular line (90-degrees) across a board. A shirt cardboard or the corner of this book lined up with the edge performs the same function.

Squaring means checking for a 90-degree angle on connected pieces of wood. A tool called a *square* (a metal ruler that looks like an *L*) or a straightedge performs this function; so does the shirt cardboard or the corner of a book.

Clamping

Holding work in place is the job of a C-clamp. Two 5″ clamps are the minimum recommended number for the small workshop. When drilling or sawing, they hold wood steady; when driving screws, they keep the holes aligned between the two pieces of wood. When gluing, they hold the surfaces just where they should

be until the glue sets. They hold miter boxes in place on the workbench. C-clamps are an invaluable tool.

Another form of "clamping" is gluing. When you have the time to let a project sit between construction steps, glue the surfaces that will eventually be nailed or screwed together. Then, when you drive in the fastener, the two pieces of wood will not separate and your bond will be doubly secure.

An optional type of clamp that is useful for tubular (pipelike) objects is a vise. If you will be handsawing dowels, a vise holds them very steadily.

Another type of clamp that is mentioned in the climber projects is a pipe clamp. With it you can clamp two pieces of wood that are a distance from one another. This can be an expensive and *optional* tool; if you already own one, then make use of it. If you are working in a group that will be making a number of climbers, then it might be a reasonable investment. Watch for a sale!

Sawing

The sawing story has two parts: there are different kinds of saws, and there are tips that make sawing easier.

The handsaw is one means of cutting lumber; it is hard work, but there are some hints that can make the job more efficient. First, practice. Second, secure the wood to the workbench with clamps so that it does not slide around. To line up a cut, draw the blade back toward your body, using your thumb to steady the saw; do this until you have a deep enough notch to proceed with the forward motion without going out of the groove. In the forward motion, the teeth do the work. Do not push so hard that the teeth bog down in the wood or so lightly that it will take forever to make a cut. Again, practice! When you get near the end of your cut, support the free piece of wood so that it does not break off and splinter. Make lighter, shorter strokes with the blade until the wood cuts cleanly.

For smaller pieces of wood like baseboard wood and dowels, the miter box is handy for sawing. The purpose of a miter box is to produce 30-, 45-, and 90-degree cuts or other precise-angle cuts. Clamp the miter box base to the workbench. Insert the wood *against* the back plate and line up the teeth of the saw with the mark for cutting. Hold the wood securely and use the same sawing

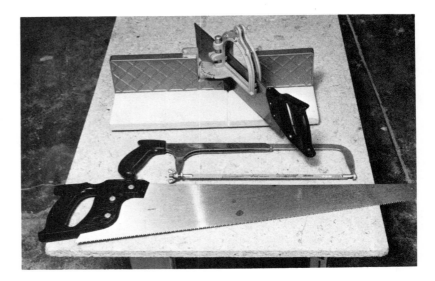

technique as with a handsaw except that the blade will be parallel to the base of the miter box (so that you do not saw through it). A good miter box is an investment well worth the cost.

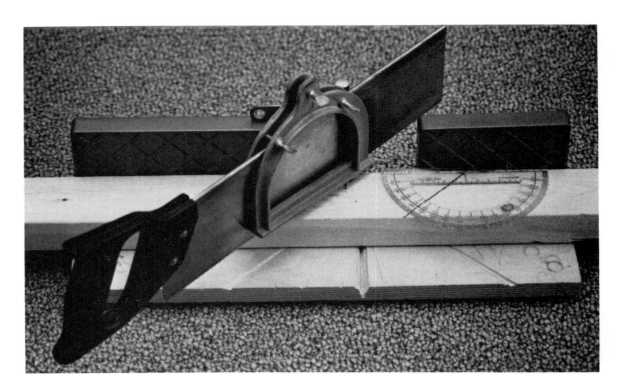

A power saw is a tool that will cut sawing time dramatically, but it is also the *most dangerous* of home tools. If you already know how to use one or if you have a carpenter who can teach you the proper technique, then take advantage of it. One way of getting around the power saw is to ask a friend with good powersawing skills to help out when you have a large amount of wood to cut. Mark all the pieces in preparation for the event. Another way is to have the large pieces, plywood, and 2×3s or 2×4s cut at the place where you bought them.

The last kind of saw mentioned in this book is a hacksaw which is used for cutting pipe. After securing the pipe with clamps or a vise, use the same directions as for the handsaw to start and finish the cut.

Sanding

Sanding is an important step in that it makes the wood as smooth as possible. Wood, by its nature, cannot be totally free from splinters, but there are some ways of minimizing them.

Experiment with the following methods of sanding to find out which feels most comfortable. Of course, the simplest method is to use sandpaper and hand power. Another way of sanding is to wrap sandpaper around a 2×2 block about 5″ long; turn the block to a different face when you need a fresh surface. The last method is to purchase a sanding block, preferably one that is made of a rubbery material that gives a little under the pressure of sanding. Medium or fine grades of paper for soft woods are good for any of the jobs described in the book. Emery paper, the black abrasive surface on clothlike paper, is not recommended for this book's projects.

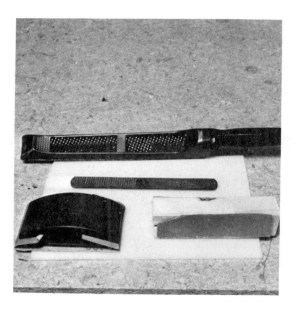

Places to sand are knots, sharp edges, drill holes, corners, and any surface that feels rough. Remove any loose wood splinters before sanding an area. The degree to which you sand depends on your judgment and on your personality! Some people are absolutely compulsive about sanding every surface, while others are pleased with a once-over. There is no right and wrong other than safety. If there is some need for filler, plastic wood putty covers the spot. If the wood is polyurethaned, the sealant covers a multitude of problems.

There are two other tools that remove rough edges or corners as does sandpaper but that are not *necessary* for any of the projects. One is a rasp, for big jobs and corners, and the other is a file, for small jobs. Use both in the same manner; push their rough surfaces away from your body and across the corner or edge to be taken off. Lift the tool off the wood; the rasp and the file are one-way tools. Dragging them back across the wood clogs them.

Drilling

There are two types of drills, hand and power. Hand drills accomplish with muscle power whatever a power drill can do, but the power drill is the only tool that will make short work of drilling holes. Drilling holes is what most of the projects call for.

Drills cost as little as $15 for a ⅜″ single-speed drill, which is adequate for all the projects in the book. There are also two-speed drills that can turn slowly or more quickly, depending on the job and type of wood. The variable-speed drill has a rheostat on the start button that can vary the speed from very slow to fast. The advantage of this is that it can be used not only for drilling all kinds of holes, but also as a power screwdriver (and as a screw remover, if it has a reverse).

The power drill holds bits that make different-size holes. A standard bit drills holes for screws and dowels from 1/16″ to ¼″. Wood drill bits are shaped like small spades with a spike, and they are sized from ⅜″ to 1½″. For the variable-speed drill, bits are available that look like screwdrivers.

To put a bit in the chuck (the prongs that open and close at the front of the drill), turn the collar around the chuck counterclockwise to loosen and insert the bit. To tighten, turn the bit clockwise; there is a geared key that inserts into the holes in the collar and turns clockwise to hold the bit securely.

The skill of drilling involves learning to drill to a specific depth and perpendicular to the wood's surface. Again, practice pays; over time you will be doing these things automatically. Drilling to a specific depth, in the beginning, takes repeated measuring of the depth of the hole. For large-diameter holes, insert a tape measure. For small-diameter holes, measure the depth of the bit in the wood against the tape. After a while you will be able to eyeball it! Another trick is to put tape around the bit just above the depth that is to be drilled; when the tape is reached, the hole is the ½″ or ¾″ depth that was marked.

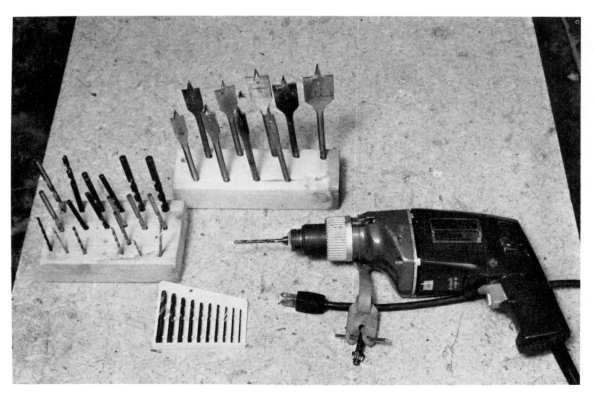

Drilling perpendicular holes, in the beginning, takes help; ask someone to look from two different directions at the angle at which you are holding the drill. He or she can correct any leaning. After a while you will get a feel for your particular machine. It might be helpful to drill what are called *tracer holes* for the large-diameter bits. Use an ⅛″ or ³⁄₁₆″ bit (with someone watching for straightness) to drill. Then the larger bit's spike has a guide for the larger cut.

Even a power drill takes some strength. Some pressure has to be put on the drill for the bit to penetrate the wood. The workbench height should be low enough that you can look down at the wood from above the drill and push down from your shoulders rather than your elbows. In the process, you should be producing sawdust; when using *wood* bits, the sawdust should be coarse and abundant. If there is not enough pressure, it will be powdery. Be careful not to rock the drill, especially when using small-diameter bits, as they will bend or break off in the hole. When removing the bit from a hole, keep the drill running until it is removed for an easier exit.

Safety is a prime consideration in the workshop. Always unplug your drill (or any other power tool) when you are finished for the day. Remove and store the bits properly—if not for their maintainence, then for your sanity the next time you are looking for a particular bit. Keep the tools out of reach of the children when you are not working with them.

Screwing

Screws come in many different kinds, sizes, and metals. The wood screw has a triangular head, a smooth shaft initially, and then a threaded shaft tapering to a point. A sheet metal screw has a round or an oval head and a totally threaded shaft tapering to a point. Both are driven with a screwdriver, either a regular screwdriver or a Phillips head screwdriver.

Wood screws come in sizes like 1×6, 2×10, ½×12. The first number is the length, measured in inches or fractions thereof. The second number represents the diameter of the shaft (the smaller the number, the smaller the diameter). Sheet metal screws also include the threads per inch in their names. Remember that the hardware person is there to help with answers and advice.

To drive a screw successfully, drill a hole first. Measure the bit against the shaft by placing the screw right under the bit; the bit should cover the shaft but not the threads. Then, when the hole is drilled and the screw inserted, the threads will bite into the wood, but the shaft will move in freely; a little glue in the hole will act as a lubricant for driving the screw and as a lock when it dries. Turn or tighten a screw just until its head is flush with the wood's surface; overtightening will cause the threads to strip the wood that is holding it in place.

When driving a wood screw into soft wood, most of the time a countersink hole is not necessary; the screw can be driven flush with the surface. (A countersink hole is a wider-diameter hole drilled at the entrance to the smaller-diameter hole to contain the head of the screw. There is a handy little drill bit sold at hardware stores that drills and countersinks all in one step; you might want to inquire about one.) Sometimes it is necessary to protect children's fingers. The hole can be filled with wood putty after the screw is in place.

Carriage bolts are smooth-headed bolts with a ¼″ threaded shaft that comes in a variety of lengths. They are held in place by a square shaped collar under the head that will not rotate in a round ¼″ hole; a washer and nut are secured at the other end. The nut end should be countersunk into the wood; this step is detailed in Agna's Climber section, construction direction 4A (see Index).

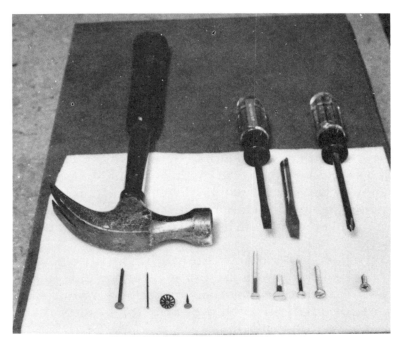

Hammering

Hammering a nail is a difficult task to do properly. Clamp the wood to a stable surface. To start the nail, hold the hammer partway up the shaft to get an accurate, short stroke on the head of the nail. A few taps should sink it enough for it to stand alone. Grasp the hammer at the handle and use harder blows to drive the nail in; the face of the hammer should be striking the nail parallel to the surface of the wood. The shorter the nail, the easier this is. Longer nails require a surer direct hit. Pressure to one side is what bends a nail.

Nails come in a variety of sizes and styles. Nails, like screws, are measured by length first and then by the diameter of the shaft. Brads are almost headless nails that can be driven into the wood for a smooth surface. Tacks are headed nails that are tapered to a very sharp point. Upholstery tacks are brads with large domed heads to hold down fabric.

Gluing

Wood glue, an ivory-colored glue, is the quick-setting kind that is recommended for the projects in the book. Dust the wood surfaces before applying the glue and use liberally. Apply a C-clamp to hold the wood in place when possible. Do not overtighten the clamp, or it will force the glue away from the surfaces. Wipe off the excess before it dries.

Polyurethaning

Polyurethane is a plastic sealant that leaves the natural beauty of the wood's grain to show, yet makes the wood washable. It is a plastic that soaks into the wood to give it a harder and more durable finish. It can seal rougher spots in wood with extra coats. Exterior grade paint covers, but it is not as durable. It is a matter of choice. In fact, for many of the projects no finish is necessary.

Polyurethane is available in paint departments and comes in a variety of sizes. The larger the size, the cheaper it is. Off-brands have the same chemical composition, so do not overspend. It takes paint thinner or mineral spirits to clean it off brushes or fingers. Use a decent-quality *soft-bristle* brush to apply it. Apply it outdoors whenever possible; it really smells awful. If it is too cold outdoors (see label for directions), apply in a well-ventilated area where the children will not smell it all day. It will make them and you cranky.

Sewing

A whipstitch is called for in a few of the cloth-covered projects. Refer to the photo for an illustration of it.

7

A PROJECT FOR THE NOVICE CARPENTER

For those of you who feel intimidated by tools, here is a special chapter. Take a deep breath and repeat a few times that this is going to be educational and *fun!* Of course the first project you take on will be the most stressful because you are entering new territory, so accept that fact and relax. Look forward to the future, when you can build that climber you want (for the children) or when you design a project yourself. It will come even though you may doubt it now. When my toy group got together, we constantly monitored each other during the early sessions, but gradually all the skills became second nature through repetition and each of us could handle the saw or drill bit with confidence. Everyone came to understand when to clamp and how to use the miter box.

You may be wondering what a miter box is. The best time to learn about a tool's function is when you use it to complete a project. You will be producing a product while you learn. Part II contains detailed instructions for using each tool. As you move through each construction direction in your chosen project, read the appropriate sections in Part II. Practice each skill once or twice on scrap wood and then complete the step in your directions.

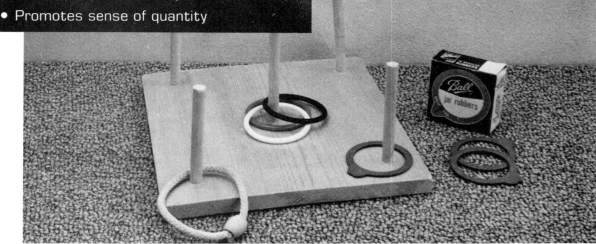

- Develops wrist movement
- Enhances eye/hand coordination
- Involves timing (through throwing motion)
- Encourages game playing
- Develops "your turn, my turn" social skills
- Promotes sense of quantity

RING TOSS

The following are instructions for materials used in and construction of the ring toss project, written especially for novice carpenters. (For the appropriate child development tips, turn to the ring toss project in Chapter 15.)

It is important to make this first effort. Your ring toss base may not be exactly square. That's OK; sawing takes practice. Maybe the pegs are not exactly perpendicular. Well, your project will still be functional, and your skills will improve over time. The important thing is that you made something to share with your children.

Specific dimensions of wood are called for that you will have to purchase; read the lumber suppliers section in Chapter 5 for starters and and then go get your supplies. The tools that you will need are fine sandpaper; wood glue; a saw; a 5" clamp; a drill, either hand or power; and a ¼" drill bit. If you also need tools, read the helpful hints in the beginning of Chapter 6.

Materials

- You need 1' of #2 pine 1×10 for the base piece. (The term *#2 pine* indicates the quality of board; *1×10* represents its dimensions, even though the wood will actually be 9" wide. All of this is explained in the lumber section of Chapter 5.)
- Dowels usually come in 3' or 4' lengths; you need one dowel that is ¼" in diameter.
- Rings can be plastic bracelets or mason jar gaskets.
- A piece of felt, 9" × 11", covers the underside of the base.

Construction

1. If the lumber supplier has precut your wood, proceed to step 3. If not, measure 12" from one end of the board at both the top and the bottom. Draw a line connecting these two points to make the sawing line.

2. Read the part on sawing in Chapter 6 and then choose a small piece of wood to practice on. Now clamp the 1×10 securely to a workbench or another stable surface. Saw on the line or as close to it as possible. Precision is not critical.

3. Measure five lengths of dowel, each 5" long. Hold them securely and cut in a miter box or on the workbench. Use the same sawing techniques that you developed in Step 2.

4. Sand all edges of your base piece and round one end of each dowel.

5. Mark a five-point pattern on the base piece for drilling. Read the section on drilling in Chapter 6 and make three practice drills in your scrap wood. Clamp down the base. Then using a ¼" drill bit, drill holes through your base piece at each mark. Since you are drilling through the board, put a scrap piece under it so that you do not drill into your work surface.

6. Put a little wood glue (described in Chapter 6) on the rough end of each dowel and insert in each hole. Wipe off the excess glue.

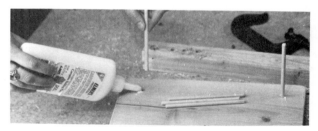

7. Cut a piece of felt for the base and glue it on the bottom side.

Congratulations! You have used the skills of measuring, sawing, clamping, drilling, and gluing; these are the major skills called for in most of the projects. You might have to reread a special tool skill section (Chapter 6) when doing the next project, but eventually it will become easy through practice.

Now enjoy the ring toss with your child and feel proud that you made it.

8
THE WOODWORKING BENCH

Whether you are working alone or with others, a place to work is essential. The project is a workbench designed for children; you can share it with them or make the legs a little longer for an adult-height surface. Just like the other projects, the woodworking bench is designed for portability and storability. It is pleasant to work outside in summer, and in the winter or in bad weather the workbench can be set up in the basement, garage, or kitchen.

Woodworking itself can be considered large-muscle work, for both children and adults. If you decide to purchase tools especially for the children, buy downsized but quality tools. Children pound and saw as hard as adults. All they really need are a small saw, a hammer, a hand drill, sandpaper, and their own bottle of glue and box of nails. They can share your C-clamps and measuring tape. Get lots of wood scraps from the lumberyard for their projects.

The bench is made with a particleboard top. It is a very hard surface and is inexpensive. The hinges on the legs in the pictures are strap hinges; actually, you should use large 4″ door hinges, which are much more stabilizing. The whole project should cost about $10 and take less than three hours to complete.

Materials

- The legs are four 22" 2×4s. If you are a tall person and are making this workbench for yourself, make the legs 28"–34" long.
- The braces across the legs are 1×8s. One piece is 30" long, and the two side pieces are 14" long each. Buy a cheap grade of wood, not good shelf board. Plywood can also be used.
- The leg frame is assembled with glue and 1½" nails or 1½"×6" screws.
- The top is a piece of ¾" particleboard measuring 24" × 40".
- The top is attached to the legs with four ¾" or 1" diameter dowels that are 1½" long.
- The hinges are two 4" fixed-pin hinges. Also needed are twelve ½" × 8" screws to attach them to the legs.
- The optional shelf is a 32" length of 1×10.

Construction

1. Cut all the wood. Sanding is not necessary, although the corners of the workbench top should be rounded.

2. Make the back leg section with two of the 2×4s and the long 1×8. Glue the brace to the legs about 8" from the bottom and clamp. Either hammer three nails into each leg or drill and insert screws.

3. Make the front leg sections in the same manner, but attach only one 2×4 to each of the 14" 1×8s.

4. Lay out the back legs section on the floor with the 2×4 side down. Lay the front leg sections on either side, lining up the 1×8 panels. (Put a scrap piece of board under the ends where the hinges will go so that the wood is on the same plane.)

5. Lay on the hinges with the pins over the space between the 1×8s and mark the spots for the drill holes. Be sure that the hinges will close flat.

6. Remove the hinges and drill the holes. Then reassemble and insert the screws.

7. Stand up the legs and drill a ¾" or 1" diameter hole for the dowels in the top of each. Drill to a depth of ¾".

8. Cut 4 dowels 1½" long and glue them into the 2×4s.

9. Lay the particleboard on the floor and put the legs on it as if the whole thing were upside down. Trace around the dowels.

10. Remove the legs and drill the appropriate-size holes (¾" or 1") in the particleboard. Because particleboard is made with glue, it will be hard to drill; put some weight on the drill. Mark this side as the wrong side for future assembly purposes.

11. Assemble the woodworking bench. Add the optional shelf by laying it across the legs, and this project is ready for the next one.

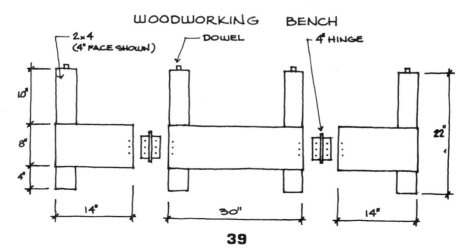

WOODWORKING BENCH

LARGE-MUSCLE EQUIPMENT

Large-muscles are the muscle groups that are exercised in activities like tumbling, hanging, jumping, climbing, and pushing. Throughout the day and evening, young children sporadically want to exercise large muscles as well as the muscles of the fingers, hands, and mouth. Since it is usually impossible to go outside every time children feel the urge to move, the ideas and plans on the following pages make it feasible to allow them large-muscle alternatives throughout their waking hours. If parents could eliminate the commands "Stop running" and "Get off the furniture" from their vocabularies, they would have a lot more time to say, "That was a good trick," or "You sure can climb."

The equipment in this book is designed to stimulate development in different groups of muscles as well as to provide engrossing playthings. The exercise mats aid in the coordination of different muscle groups. The doorway gym mainly develops upper torso strength, while the climbers mainly improve lower body strength. The walking and balance boards and the jumping equipment help children develop different skills associated with balance. The streamers and ring toss help them develop arm and wrist movement. The wheel toys stimulate the pushing and pulling muscle groups, while the hobbyhorse and soft blocks are for general movement and fun. All the above stimulate pretend play!

When rethinking a household system to include large-muscle equipment, you should first develop a plan. Estimate the amount of space that can be created for climbers and doorway gyms *and* their storage places. Another consideration is the *present* age and abilities of the children. A final consideration is budget. Although the homemade equipment is not expensive, buying the lumber in one lump sum may be difficult.

Pace your plans, looking at your needs and setting up priorities for projects. Once all of the top-priority projects have been built, remember that they do not all have to be in the environment at one time. Overstimulation is tough on children; deciding among three activities is easier than deciding among ten, and it is a lot safer to have a less dense play space.

Although the top priority might be a climber, if you have never worked with tools, start with an easy project like a walking board or a ring toss, then try climber accessories like a ladder and slide. Part II presents helpful hints for using tools and choosing lumber. Since the major material called for is wood, it is wise to learn about it before proceeding with a project.

There are some general rules that apply to all the construction directions:

1. Sand all wood smooth of splinters.

2. Round the corners so that there are no sharp points sticking out.

3. Seal wood that will be heavily used with polyurethane.

4. Safety is a foremost consideration.

5. Finally, ask for help when you need it. There is no such thing as a dumb question when it will help you make a better, safer product.

9
THE EXERCISE MATS

The exercise mat is a basic piece of equipment. Its primary function is for jumping and tumbling, but mats can be used for a variety of other functions. They can be used in combination with other equipment to create new spaces, to cushion climbers, or just as part of the decor of the room. There are many uses for exercise mats, beginning in the baby years and continuing throughout childhood.

Children usually begin to have a need to jump and tumble after they have completed the developmental tasks of learning to walk well, to run, and to execute a two-footed jump. When they have conquered the upright skills, they turn to whole-body experimentation. Jumping is momentarily defying gravity, while tumbling is acquiescing to it. (It is wonderful that children naturally teach themselves certain physics lessons.) The somersault is one of the first tumbling procedures children attempt at around two and a half years of age. It is a feat of skill and bravery because they are placing their weight on the neck and shoulders, a totally new experience.

When the child has learned this tumble, another one to master is the fall and roll. Some children learn this procedure through athletic coaching, and learning it can spare them from many a bruise. When falling forward, the child tucks the chin and rolls onto one shoulder. Continuing the roll, the child uses his or her arm, first curled at the chest to push off the mat and then through the somersault. It is a skill that will be helpful in adulthood when falls are usually more traumatic. If adults, especially women, could tuck and roll, it might save breaking an arm or wrist.

When the exercise mat is not being used for acrobatics, it can serve other needs. It can be stored under the climber and therefore serve as a protection against falls. It can be stored in a cozy corner and become a place to curl up with a good book or for a nap. On a platform, the exercise mat can double as a bed. It can be a baby climber or soft blocks (both are described later). Some larger, more bulky exercise mats have permanent spots in a child's environment; these spots can be located next to climbers or under doorway gyms and still allow for tumbling as well as serving as protection.

PORTABLE MATS

A key consideration when making, buying, or improvising a portable mat is the child's ability to haul it about the space. If it is bulky, heavy, or both, children are less likely to use it creatively and to put it where it belongs at the end of their activity. Several easily obtainable materials make good movable mats.

Crib mattresses are the largest mat that the four- or five-year-old can handle. Covering the mattress protects it from being ripped by buckles and other sharp objects. It is springy for jumping and just the right size for tumbling.

Urethane foam, another mat material, can be purchased in a variety of shapes, sizes, and thicknesses at department, discount, and dry goods stores. If a special size is needed to fit a platform, for example, it can be made to order by a manufacturer (look in the Yellow Pages under "Plastics—Foam") or more cheaply cut to fit with a serrated knife. (See the project titled "Soft Blocks" for cutting details.) For general use as a napping place, roof, mat, etc., a 4" thickness is ideal. One mat pictured is 22" × 42" × 4"; it is stiff yet pliable and portable. If the exercise mat is also being used as a bed, a 6" thickness is quite comfortable.

There are numerous ways to cover a mat, but the easiest, especially for non-sewers, is to wrap the fabric like a birthday present and whipstitch the entire seam with heavy thread. Denim, corduroy, and upholstery fabric are the best covers. Although vinyl would be ideal for cleanability, it requires "professional" upholstering and is not very comfortable for cuddling.

47

NONPORTABLE MATS

Some mats have special functions and fixed places; they are not meant to be portable. They need to be placed so that they are not in family traffic patterns. For example, fixed mats are useful under climbers, especially when new or belonging to that daring toddler or preschooler. Trapezes, rings, and toddler swings are other pieces of equipment that might need a fixed mat underneath for safety. Sometimes children have a special need to bounce on a mattress. If the bed is off-limits, then providing a large mattress will satisfy that urge while sparing the furniture.

Mattresses or futons covered with fitted sheets or heavy fabric can be used as permanent padding. They can be stored under a climber or find a home outside on a weather-protected porch or in a basement. Another extrathick area for tumbling or protection can be made from two or three pieces of old carpet basted or glued on top of each other. Double-sided carpet tape keeps carpet squares in place on slippery flooring. Another soft material for large areas is rug or carpet padding folded into four (or more) thicknesses and covered with a sheet or other facric.

Each environment, whether bedroom, basement, outdoor space, or family room, will have some way to incorporate an exercise mat into the design. The mat can be used for its own sake, jumping and tumbling, or in conjunction with other needs and equipment, beds, and climbers.

- Enhances coordination of muscle groups
- Promotes balance
- Develops sense of orientation in space
- Reduces fear of different body orientations

BUSE'S MAT

This portable, storable mat serves both a tumbling and a safety function. It is small enough to be handled by a three- or four-year-old and is easy enough to be made by any mom or dad.

Materials

- The foam is urethane available at discount and sewing stores; it is 2" thick and 22" × 76".
- The covering is made from corduroy, although any heavy fabric such as denim or cotton upholstery material will suffice. The material will have to be twice the length of the foam plus 6"; in this case, (76 × 2) + 6 = 158" or 4½ yards.
- The fasteners are Velcro strips; strips provide a larger surface area for fastening power than a small circle of Velcro sewn to a ribbon. About 2" of adhesive surface can hold the foam when it is curled up. Velcro is widely available in sewing departments and also in large hardware departments.

Construction

Hand Sewing

1. Folding the material into two equal lengths, lay it out on a large spot of open floor; place the foam on top. Trim the fabric, leaving 3″ of extra material all around the foam. (You will now have two separate pieces of fabric).

2. Assemble the three layers (fabric, foam, and fabric) as they will be sewn together. Fold the edges ½″ and then refold one more inch; pin as you work.

3. Whipstitch all four seams (along the edges of the mat) closed with heavy-duty thread, removing the pins as you work. (See Part II for an explanation of this stitch).

4. When finished, roll the mat up and pin the Velcro strips where they will lap over the end seam as pictured in the photograph. Unroll the mat and sew on the Velcro with ample stitches, using heavy-duty thread.

Machine Sewing

1. Lay out the two pieces of fabric, right sides together, and place the foam on top. Trim the fabric, leaving 3″ of extra material all around the foam.

2. Mark the hem 1½″ from the edge of the foam and, removing the foam, pin the fabric together on two long sides and one short side.

3. Insert the rough half of the Velcro strips in the pinned end seams about 7″ from the sides. Make sure that the strips will extend from the seam when you turn the fabric right side out.

4. Machine stitch (preferably zigzag) the short end of the mat with the Velcro twice. Machine stitch the side seams.

5. Turn the cover right side out as you insert the foam.

6. Put open edges together and fold twice; whipstitch closed.

7. Roll up the mat and pin the Velcro where it will meet the rough strips. Hand sew in place with heavy-duty thread.

10
THE DOORWAY GYM

A swing—inside! This has been one of the most exciting pieces of equipment tested by the children. It is such a simple idea and a simple procedure to attach a swing, trapeze, or any of the other equipment in this chapter to a door frame. Young children concentrate on swinging, while the older ones delight in experimenting with new ways to position themselves in space. The pendulum motion of a swing stimulates the senses of balance, acceleration/deceleration, and kinesthesia. The development of upper body strength through the hanging apparatus like the rope ladder or knotted/beaded rope is an added benefit. The tetherball and punching bag satisfy the hitting needs in a positive way.

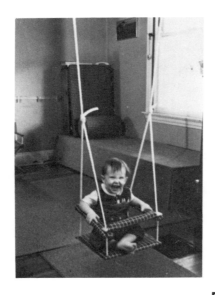 

SAFETY

The first consideration with the doorway gym equipment is safety for both the user and the other members of the family. Ground rules established on the *first day* it is installed are one of the best safety measures. A list of possible rules to choose from include:

Swing straight.

One at a time.

Swingers (over 3) are responsible for not swinging into others.

No chairs to climb on the rings, trapeze, or rope ladder.

Use a mat under certain equipment.

One apparatus gets put away before another is put up.

An adult must be present.

A rule not included in this list is: Share the equipment. It may seem incongruous, but children who have things taken away from them find it difficult to share; they are on their guard to retain possession. It is better to create an atmosphere in which children can swing or hang until they are tired of it. This promotes attention span and an awareness of their state of mind (and body) as well as demotes the attitude that they are losing something and must hang on at all costs. This new atmosphere takes a long time to build if the old attitude has to fade first. In the meantime, to reduce tension, a parent can use an egg timer, an hourglass, or the big hand of the clock to let the children decide when their turns are over. Increasing the intervals over a couple of weeks may allow the child to get tired of swinging within a given turn and relinquish the seat on his or her own. Since the equipment is portable, it can be put away if rules are not followed or the procedure of taking turns is not resolved by the children.

The rule about swingers' responsibilities is a problem. When there is more than one user, all children have to learn not to swing into companions and not to walk in front of the swinger. This is an especially hard lesson for toddlers to learn because they do not have the cognitive capacity to understand the cause/effect relationship until it has been reinforced a couple of times through hard knocks. Adults have to be especially careful of and for this age group.

There is a fine line between experimentation and "horsing around" and between learning from bumps and hurting oneself. Children, as they master skills, will attempt new feats; it is a natural process of development. Some children are cautious by nature, while others seem less aware of their own safety. Each adult, with these points in mind, will have to make a determination about

the child's abilities, supervising the work, and enforcing some rules. This job will be easier for the child who grows up with the equipment; the children just introduced to it will not know the extent of their limitations and strength and the physical laws of swinging, hanging, etc. It will take them some time to become nonchalant about the doorway gym.

CHOOSING A LOCATION

The best place to locate the gym is in a doorway near where the children play (or where you want them to play). For the most part, children like to work near adults. So, if you want to provide engrossing activities for the children, it's best to locate the gym near the area you are likely to spend your time in. For example, in the evening, when adults like to relax, a doorway off the living room is the best choice. Socialization with Mom and Dad is highly important to young children. The children who tested the equipment for this book chose play sites near adults. For the most part, they played "in their rooms or down in the basement" when they had age mates over to play, but each family has its own style.

Another consideration for placement is the household traffic pattern. One father almost knocked the wind out of himself walking into a tension bar across the kitchen door, and it is nerve-wracking to constantly dodge a swinger while setting the table for dinner. Since the doorway gym is portable, not a permanent fixture, it can have different homes for different times of the day. It can be taken down when company comes, when passage through a doorway is necessary, or when it cannot be supervised properly.

Safe doorways are located away from stairs, glass doors, jutting furniture, lamps, and other potentially dangerous or breakable objects. The maximum arc that is produced by an older child swinging in a seven foot doorway is about seven feet on either side of the frame; baby swings and rope climbers have significantly smaller arcs.

SETTING UP THE DOORWAY GYM

After deciding on safe doorways, the next step is to attach the gym to a door frame. An archway is an ideal location because the gym will not block the whole egress. But often the middle of a frame is hollow. For an arch or any doorway, the recommended method is to use heavy-duty hooks (like those on which a porch swing would be hung) screwed into the framing. Test for hollowness by knocking. Find a solid place in the lintel or in one side of the frame (for less visible hooks) at least ½" from the edge. Drill the holes ¹⁄₁₆" narrower than the diameter of the shaft of the hook into the wood or drywall as deep as the threads on the hook. Screw in the hooks until the threads are no longer visible. A little white glue on the threads acts first as a lubricant and then as a lock, but the hooks are still removable.

The above method of attaching the doorway gym is not always feasible, especially in rented homes. Some landlords will give permission if the damage is repaired when the tenant moves. To repair the holes after the screws are removed, or to repair any other damage to woodwork, fill with wood putty, sand the surface smooth, and repaint or stain the spot.

Another attachment method that is especially good for metal joists that are in basements or in thin door frames involves the use of C-clamps. Large, heavy-duty ones can be expensive, but when the equipment is well used over a period of years, the investment is worth it. Position the clamps as pictured and attach the ropes.

A third method for installing the doorway gym, which can be used in a 28″–36″ door frame, is to use a tension bar with an adult weight capacity. Tension bars are sold in sporting goods departments; attach according to manufacturer's suggestions. They are a fun piece of equipment by themselves as well. When the bar is secured at waist, chest, or head height, the child can do flips, chin-ups, and other tricks.

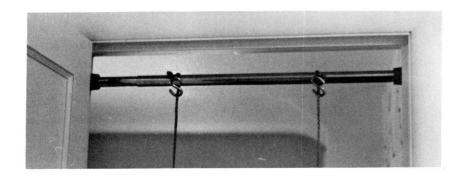

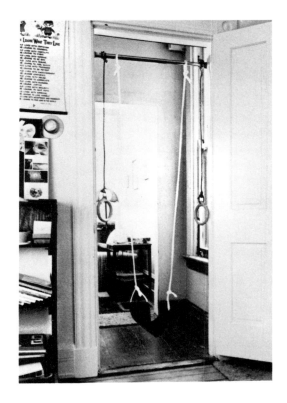

After deciding on a safe system, the next step is to choose the appropriate equipment for the developmental abilities of your child. The following sections, describing each piece of equipment, are listed in ascending order of difficulty and contain an explanation of the kinds of skills and strengths needed to use each.

Introducing a piece of equipment before the child has the skill to use it could lead to accidents, fear of trying new tricks, and frustration, not to mention a damaged ego. Children may not use the gym, and this defeats the purpose of providing them with enthralling play equipment. Be careful to separate your own enthusiasm for what you have made or your childhood fantasies about swinging from the reality of your child's abilities and common sense.

One piece of equipment that should not be used in the doorway gym is a disk swing; that is a plate centered on a single rope. It is free-swinging and rotates in a circle instead of back and forth. Often children lean back and their heads become rams; it is a very difficult swing to control and therefore is not recommended.

Another consideration in setting up the gym is storage for the extra rings, tetherball, etc. Because the equipment has ropes that can tangle if stored in a bin or toy box, it is better to hang the equipment from an extra hook or a rack. A 1×2 drilled to accept a few short 1½″ dowels or an expandable cup rack sold at the discount stores holds the ropes tangle-free.

All the equipment must be checked regularly for safe use; look for cracks, fraying, tears, or loose parts. Remove and repair or replace damaged material. Since you made it, you are familiar with all the materials and their construction.

ROPE

The rope used for the doorway gym equipment is ⅜″ *hollow-core nylon rope;* solid-core rope is also appropriate, but it is stiffer and harder to knot. Both are available at hardware stores, discount stores, department stores, and marine outlets and cost 10¢–35¢ a foot, depending on the store. Shop around for the best price. Nylon rope is strong, lightweight, and does not cause "splinters" like hemp rope, so little fingers are safe.

The measurements for the length of rope needed for each piece of gym equipment are based on their being hung in a 7′ doorway. If your door frame or ceiling is higher, adjust the lengths accordingly. Some lengths are purposely long, the trapeze, for example, so that they can be hung at swing height as well as 3′ or 4′ off the ground. Continually adjust the heights as your children grow or as their skills demand it. Remember to check the rope regularly for damage.

For those who were not scouts, a simple self-tightening knot is illustrated. It is easily adjusted to level out the seat of the trapeze or change the heights of the equipment. It is the knot used to hang the doorway gym, the big triangle of the baby swing, and the small triangle of the soft swing.

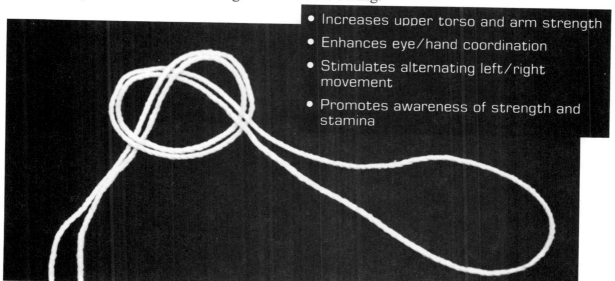

- Increases upper torso and arm strength
- Enhances eye/hand coordination
- Stimulates alternating left/right movement
- Promotes awareness of strength and stamina

- Provides experience in acceleration/deceleration
- Promotes interaction with parent

BABY SWING

There are windup infant swings on the market that swing "indefinitely" and are supposed to take care of baby while Mom or Dad has other things to do. This swing is not one of those! First, it is designed for the seven- to twenty-four-month-old; second, it has to be pushed regularly; and third, it has to be attended. The reward is the parent-child interaction. It is a great early game in depth perception and anticipation as baby swings first toward Mom or Dad's face and then away, having his toes tickled with each advance. And this swing does not need a lot of space because babies do not like to swing very high. Baby swing models are commercially available for $12–$30; the one pictured here cost about $2 plus the cost of the rope.

Materials

- The seat is a 12"×12" piece of plywood or pine board at least ⅜" thick.
- The side pieces are 1¾" lattice (a type of baseboard wood). A 1×2 will also work. Four 12" pieces are needed.
- You need 24' of rope to let it swing.

Construction

1. Begin with the 12″×12″ board; drill four ⅜″ holes, one through each corner, about ¾″ from the edges.

2. Cut four pieces of lattice the same length as the base (in this case 12″) and drill two ⅜″ holes through each, ¾″ from the ends.

3. Either sand all edges very smooth or cover the wood with cloth. The swing pic-tured has each piece of wood wrapped in foam and then rewrapped with material; seams are whipstitched. Slits are then cut in the fabric where each drilled hole is.

4. Thread a 12′ nylon rope on each side, following the numbered steps in the diagram, and knot into a triangle as pictured. Repeat on the other side.

THREADING DIAGRAM FOR THE SIDE VIEW OF THE BABY SWING

1. KNOT
2. SIDE SUPPORT
3. BACK SUPPORT
4. KNOT

5. SEAT

11. DOUBLE ROPE KNOT

10. FRONT BAR SUPPORT

9. KNOT
8. SIDE SUPPORT

7. KNOT

6. SEAT

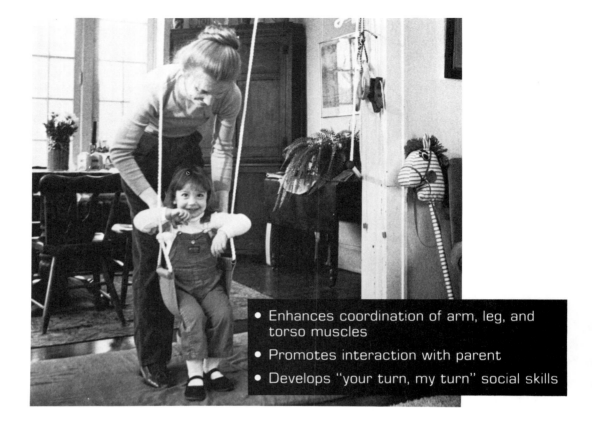

- Enhances coordination of arm, leg, and torso muscles
- Promotes interaction with parent
- Develops "your turn, my turn" social skills

SOFT SWING

For swinging, twirling, or even just sitting, this piece of equipment is very popular with children. The swing hugs the child's bottom and provides a soothing rocking motion.

Toddlers should start with a soft swing that has a back on the seat and padding on the floor. Young children usually fall off two or three times before they learn the skill of swinging, so taking precautions is necessary. You may want to put an exercise mat under the swing. After a number of weeks with no spills, the back can be removed with a seam ripper, but you should continue to use the padding for some time.

The soft swing has a light and snug seat that is difficult to slide out of. Another plus is that it is lightweight and does not hurt much when it hits a child in the head. Swings that are sold for backyard swing sets are inexpensive, but for an indoor space and for preschoolers they are not recommended. One reason is that they are more difficult to balance; children often slide off the plastic seats. The other reason is that they hurt when they hit a child in the head.

The swing needs a large, clear path in which to make its arc; five to seven feet on either side of the door must be free of obstacles. If your house does not have this amount of space, skip the swing and provide other large-muscle alternatives in the doorway with a rope ladder, beaded rope, or tension bar (all described later in this chapter). As a safety measure in a narrow door space, children must be reminded often to swing straight; if the rule is not followed, then the equipment can be taken down as a natural consequence of not following the safety guidelines.

To cost out the soft swing, it takes only about $1 worth of aluminum or plastic PVC pipe, $4 worth or rope, and the cost, if any, of the fabric for the seat. (The catch with aluminum pipe is that you must buy six feet of it. In order to use it all, share it with others in a toy group, make a trapeze with the extra, or construct other swings and give them as gifts.)

Materials

- Two 6" lengths of 1" diameter aluminum pipe are the rope holders for the swing. The trapeze calls for the same aluminum pipe, which is sold in 6' lengths in the hardware department; it is ¾"–1" in diameter and .047"–.057" in wall thickness. Be careful *not* to buy clothes closet poling, which has a seam running down its length. (Heavy-duty plastic PVC pipe will also work. Large hardware stores carry 6" lengths in about a 1" diameter.)
- The seat and back, if any, are made of ½ yard of heavy fabric such as denim, corduroy, or outdoor canvas material.
- You need eighteen feet of rope to form the swing.

Construction

1. Cut a piece of heavy corduroy, denim, or other heavy fabric approximately 24" × 13"; if the child weighs over fifty pounds, the fabric may be 28" or 30" × 13".

2. Fold right sides together to form a seat 24" × 6½". Machine zigzag stitch the open long edge. (A straight stitch acts like a perforated line, and the cloth rips easily.)

3. Turn the tube inside out. Fold the ends over so that the pipes will fit snugly and zigzag two or three times.

4. Cut two 6" lengths of 1" diameter aluminum pipe with a hacksaw. File away any rough points.

5. Insert the pipes; then thread two 9' ropes through the pipes and knot to form triangles near the seat. Use electrician's or masking tape to wrap any loose rope ends.

6. Optional: If a back is needed, cut another piece of fabric approximately 10" × 6". Again fold right sides together to form a 10" × 3" back and stitch; turn right side out. Attach each end to the swing just below the pipes. Use a large zigzag stitch so that it can be removed easily when the back is no longer needed.

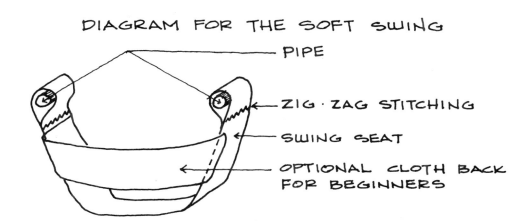

DIAGRAM FOR THE SOFT SWING

PIPE

ZIG·ZAG STITCHING

SWING SEAT

OPTIONAL CLOTH BACK FOR BEGINNERS

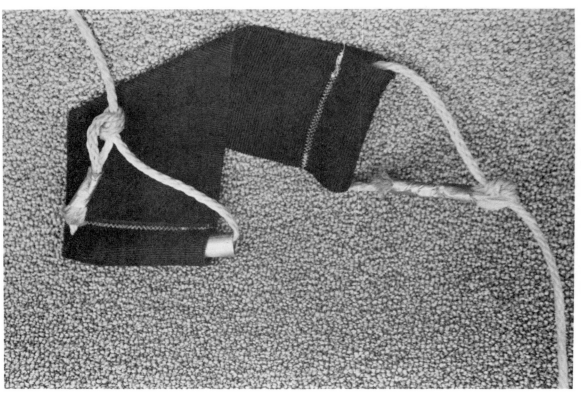

TRAPEZE AND RINGS

The purpose of the trapeze and rings is the development of upper body strength through hanging. Arm strength lags behind the development of leg strength in young children.

For the most part, children over four are the ones who use the hanging equipment to flip and do other tricks, but the two- and three-year-olds also love to use them to turn around and around and then spin freely. They get so dizzy that you have to take care that they don't bump into furniture. (There are two extremes of behavior for which parents should be wary in a toddler/preschooler, conditions which you should mention to your child's physician. The first is the child who cannot tolerate any amount of spinning or vestibular stimulation, and the second is the child who can spin for minutes on end without stopping or who does not display dizziness when finished.) Another feat that the younger set likes to do with both rings and trapeze is to run, grasp, and swing. Since the child is hanging directly under the equipment, there is no danger of banging into the door frame with the head as the child might do on the soft swing.

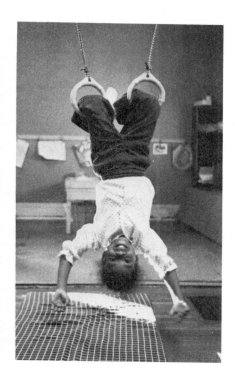

TRAPEZE

Adults need to be patient with the time it takes to become a skilled aerialist. The trapeze should first be hung at swing height to help the child develop a sense of balance on such a thin seat; then it can be raised to hanging height to work on the arm/chest muscles. Children, when they are ready, will combine the skills necessary for getting on the trapeze three feet off the ground. That is sometime after the age of four.

A good ground rule for the trapeze is: If you can't get on it yourself, you can't (and shouldn't) be up that high. Resist the temptation to lift children onto the trapeze. Once they have been up there, they will want to be lifted up often, and that is not independent work. If they can get up on the trapeze, then it is a logical assumption that they have the strength and balance to do their tricks safely. You will want to place an exercise mat underneath the equipment.

Trapezes are easy to make; the one pictured is made of aluminum pipe and is very strong yet lightweight. It also has rope sides that are easier on young hands than chain. The trapeze costs about $7 if made with aluminum piping. The piping is described in detail in the materials section of the soft swing. It can also be made with wood doweling for slightly less; both construction directions are given so that you can choose, depending on the materials that you have available.

Materials

- Either 16" of aluminum piping or 16" of 1" diameter wood dowel forms the seat.
- You need 16' of rope for the sides.
- Two crutch tips or chair leg covers, the same diameter as the pipe or dowel, cushion the ends of the trapeze.

Construction

Aluminum Trapeze

1. Cut a 16" length of ¾"–1" diameter aluminum pipe (.047"–.057" wall thickness) with a hacksaw.

2. Clamp the pipe securely or put it in a vise. Drill a ⅜" diameter hole through one wall on each end. Then file all rough edges.

3. Thread an 8' nylon rope, with the ends wrapped in tape, through the drilled hole, into the pipe, and out through the other hole; then knot it. Stuff the knot into the pipe, tugging so it is secure. Repeat on the other side.

4. Cover the pipe ends with crutch tips or chair leg caps.

Wooden Trapeze

1. Cut 16" of 1" diameter dowel.

2. Clamp securely or put the dowel in a vise. Drill two small-diameter starter holes through the dowel about ¾" from each end. Have someone help you line up the drill for straight holes. Then redrill the holes using a ⅜" drill bit; sand the bar and the ends smooth.

3. Cut the 16' of rope into two 8' lengths. Thread each rope through one of the holes and knot the ends until they cannot be pulled through the holes. To tie a large knot, make a loop with the rope and, instead of putting the free end through one time, recircle it through two or three times and then pull tightly.

4. Tape the fraying ends of the rope so that they do not unravel.

5. Optional: Cover the ends with crutch tips or chair leg caps.

- Increase arm strength (to support body weight)
- Increase leg strength
- Enhance coordination of muscle groups
- Promote awareness of strength and stamina

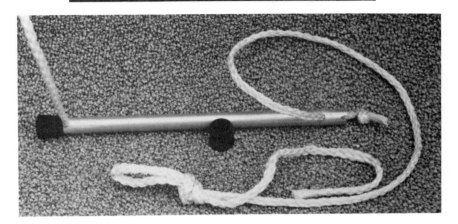

RINGS

The rings are a step up in difficulty. They require much the same skills as the trapeze, but they are harder to mount. Back and then front flips are perfected first. The coordination needed to get the feet into and out of the rings while hanging is a skill that most children develop later, usually around age six. The exercise mat is a must for these fancy feats.

Homemade versions of this doorway gym item were very unsuccessful. Instead, they were purchased at one of those large chain toy stores that carry almost everything; they are easier to find in spring and summer. The best ones are plastic; they are strong yet lightweight and cost only $4. Weightier models are available at a slightly higher cost, but they also hurt a little more if a child is bumped in the head by them. If they come with chains, the chains can be replaced by nylon rope which won't be as hard on children's hands.

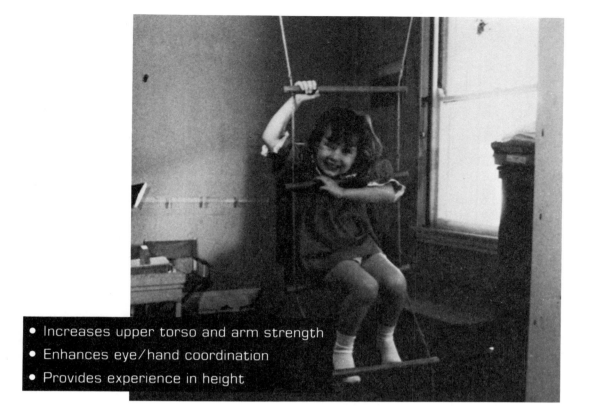

- Increases upper torso and arm strength
- Enhances eye/hand coordination
- Provides experience in height

ROPE LADDER

The rope ladder is the recommended next step in the doorway gym apparatus and is intended for children at least three or four years old. It can be used as a swing, for sitting; as a trapeze, for hanging; or as a climber, for developing upper body strength. For children who do not have the ability to pull themselves up on a trapeze three to four feet off the ground, the rope ladder provides a means of getting this high without an adult's help. It does not have a wide seat like a swing, so it encourages the kinds of balancing skills necessary to use a piece of equipment like the trapeze. The rope ladder provides the child with a huge number of possibilities to explore. For safety, you may want to put an exercise mat under the equipment.

Children love to pretend they are circus performers, fire fighters, or house painters. They love to test their strength and balance through climbing, and they love to be "taller" than Mom or Dad once they reach the upper rungs. Remember to place the exercise mat underneath for children new to the rope ladder.

When used as a climbing and hanging apparatus, the rope ladder does not require a great deal of space. As a swing, it does need five to six feet on either side of the opening, but be aware that the free rungs under the swinger whip back and forth. It is an inexpensive investment, about $7.

Materials

- Five or six 16″ lengths of 1″ or 1¼″ diameter wood doweling are the rungs.
- Two 9′–10′ lengths of rope are needed.

Construction

1. Cut the rungs and sand smooth. Polyurethaning is optional.

2. Clamp each dowel securely to the workbench or hold in a vise. Drill starter holes with a ⅛" bit through the dowels about ¾" from each end. Have someone help in eyeing the drill so that you get a straight hole. Then redrill the holes using a ⅜" drill bit; sand or file all rough edges.

3. Starting with the bottom rung, thread two 9'–10' ropes through each hole of the first rung and knot below the dowel. Reknot on the other side of the rung to keep the child from moving the rods up and down, fraying the rope. If a larger knot is needed to hold the rung, then thread the rope through the loop of the knot two or three times to increase its bulk.

4. Knot the rope about 8"–10" above this rung to form the base knot for the next rung. Keep the ropes taut to make sure all knots are spaced evenly; they can be loosened, slipped up or down, and retightened if adjustment is needed. Add the second rung and continue the procedure until all rungs are in place. Hang the rope ladder, either by using S-hooks (as shown in photos) or by making loops in the ends of the rope (as explained in the beginning of the doorway gym section). Enjoy!

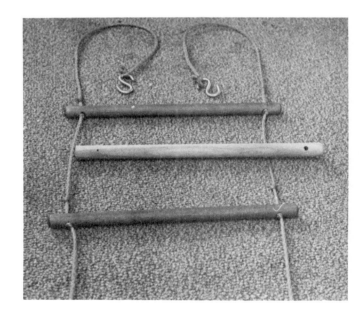

- Increases upper torso and arm strength
- Enhances eye/hand coordination
- Stimulates alternating left/right movement
- Promotes awareness of strength and stamina

KNOTTED/BEADED ROPE

The knotted rope is a hangover from high school gym days! It takes a great deal of upper body strength to hang or to draw up one's own weight, hand over hand, so this is usually for older children. (Since a child might overestimate his strength and fall or have to jump down from the rope, placing an exercise mat underneath might be a good idea.) Also, it is the one piece of equipment that is free-swinging; it does not just move back and forth but rotates 360 degrees. For Tarzan-type tricks, which even younger children like to do, it should be hung in an open space, such as from a basement joist, an archway, or the porch ceiling. Younger children who had older siblings who used the rope found a great deal of satisfaction when they could finally conquer this piece of equipment.

Materials

- The only nonoptional material is 9' of nylon rope. All the other doorway gym pieces call for ⅜" rope; this is OK to use, but a ½" rope is a little easier to grasp.
- Beads or spools that thread over the rope are optional.

Construction

1. Construction is simple. Double-knot about every 6″ to 9″ a 9′ length of heavy nylon rope. Placing a bead or large spool between knots is optional.

2. Loop the end and knot to hang.

MORE FOR THE DOORWAY GYM

Indoors or out, the tetherball and punching bag are accessories for the doorway gym that are fun for the toddler, preschooler, and parent. They promote eye-hand coordination, which is necessary not only for athletic skills but also for academic skills such as writing. As with the other gym equipment, these additions are portable and storable, and they cost virtually nothing to make.

- Enhances eye/hand coordination
- Stimulates catching motion
- Develops "your turn, my turn" social skills

TETHERBALL

For young children, a ball on a string provides a toy that cannot roll under the sofa or out into the street. They can throw it or bat at it to their hearts' content, and it will always come back. This is a valuable lesson; children learn to anticipate the ball's coming back to them.

The doorway gym tetherball is excellent for children who are learning to catch. As the ball swings to the top of its arc, it stops momentarily, and this makes it easy to grasp, whereas a thrown ball does not necessarily stop at the fingertips. A child who has a visual impairment can use a ball with a bell inside to provide extra sensorial stimulation for locating the target.

The tetherball game variations are numerous, depending on the ball size, texture and weight, and on the players. One two-year-old has a whiffleball on a string, and he and Dad play their own version of indoor baseball. Rules can be made up for indoor soccer, tetherball, etc. Be aware though, that the ball swings as high as the ceiling in all directions, so try out the game before the children do to survey what is breakable within the radius of the ball.

Materials

- To make the tetherball, buy some fruit at the grocery store in a plastic, expandable net bag. Eat the fruit!
- Pick one of the balls lying around the house.
- Cord or rope about 8' long ties it up.

Construction

1. If the bag is not already knotted, do so. Turn the net bag inside out so that the fringed end is not exposed. Insert any ball, gather the extra netting, and make a loop or knot.

2. Tie securely a number of times with heavy cord or rope.

3. Put loops along the cord and at the end for different ball heights when hung.

- Enhances eye/hand coordination
- Provides aggression release

PUNCHING BAG

Whether you are training Rocky VII, have an aggressive child who needs a nonhuman outlet, or just have children who like to punch, the punching bag is perfect. It can be hung from the doorway gym. It might not be used as much spontaneously as it is used at Mom's suggestion, "Oh, I see you need to pound on something," or "*This* is made for hitting." Pounding is an activity practiced by *both* sexes.

Make a bag of whatever size you need. The one pictured is an adult's pants leg cut off above the knee and stitched closed at the bottom. A soft fabric stuffing, well packed, is appropriate for young knuckles. If you use the pants leg idea, take up the construction directions with Step #2.

Materials

- The bag is constructed from 24″ × 24″ fabric.
- You need 5″ of strong ribbon or binding to connect bag and rope.
- The stuffing can be old clothes, towels, fabric scraps, pillow stuffing, etc. (as long as there are no zippers, buttons, snaps, or other hard sharp objects in the fabric).
- A 5′ rope holds the punching bag.

Construction

1. Fold material in half with right sides together. Sew up the open side seam of the bag.

2. Stitch a ½" hem in what will be the bottom of the bag. Sew the bottom according to the diagram below.

3. Turn inside out and stuff.

4. Stitch closed at the top in the same fashion as the bottom.

5. Sew on a loop of strong ribbon with ample stitches.

6. Attach a rope and hang from the doorway gym.

PANTSLEG . . . . . . FOLD . . . . STITCH

11
CLIMBERS

It's easy to imagine a climber at the park or in a backyard, and it's also easy to imagine children climbing on furniture. Combining the two thoughts gives rise to the indoor climber!

Children need to exercise muscles on rainy days, cold days, mornings, afternoons. A climber not only saves furniture and provides an outlet for pent-up energy but also offers children a place to strengthen large muscle groups, those muscles of the arms and legs that are used for gross movement. They experiment with new sensations, tension in different parts of the body, and positions in space. A climber also offers something often overlooked, a new, higher, or even upside-down view of a familiar world; children need to experience seeing from different perspectives.

Besides the advantage of large-muscle stimulation, the climber offers children a prop upon, around, or under which they can imagine. It can be a rocket, fire engine, grocery store, school, etc. Covered, it can be a place to hide all alone or share with family and friends. As children grow from the toddler years, when pretending is prop-dependent and short-lived, to the later preschool years, when it is long-lived and imagination takes the place of props, pretending becomes an hour of drama with a consistent cast of characters. The climber can be part of this action.

Whatever the need, pretend or movement, plans for climbers and accessories that go with them are outlined on the following pages. They have a variety of features and you should consider height, portability, variability, and design (including slant and strength) in choosing one for your environment.

Obviously, the younger the child, the lower the climber should be, but even for the oldest child the height limit should be five feet. (The U.S. government published a report on playground safety and found that most serious falling

injuries, especially head injuries, occur on equipment over that height, regardless of the surface on which the child falls.) Most of the plans in this book call for four-foot limits, and children from age two to seven have found this both stimulating and safe.

The next feature is portability. This aspect of the climber designs is necessary because moving is a fact of modern life. All the homemade climbers pictured have seen their owners change residences, two cross-country, but portability is also important for other reasons. In small homes and apartments a climber can take up a large amount of square footage. When company comes, when the equipment is being misused, or when other toys or games demand the space, most of the climbers can be folded up and stored behind a bookcase, under a bed, or in a closet. Some can be moved from bedroom to basement to family room without a great deal of hassle. Portable climbers can also go outside on the porch or in the yard on sunny days; renters who cannot erect permanent outdoor equipment can still provide an exciting outdoor space.

The person who does all this moving does not necessarily have to be Mom or Dad; older children can handle most of the equipment. And the fact that the climbers and accessories are detachable and lightweight gives them great variability. Children can create spaces. They can experiment with different heights, slants, widths, closures, etc. This feature is rarely found in large-muscle apparatus; public playgrounds and even traditional backyard swing sets do not offer children a chance to manipulate the whole environment. There is a separate section for climber accessories at the end of this chapter so that you can look over the possibilities and choose the ones that are appropriate for your climber, your budget, and your child's abilities.

Design is another consideration in choosing or modifying climbers. One feature of the designs is the degree of slant in the ladders. Climbing vertically transfers much of the body's weight to the arms; climbing on a slanted or more horizontal surface has the opposite effect. It puts the weight on the legs while the arms are used for balance. The child under age three has a more well-developed set of muscles in the lower body and therefore finds it easier to climb on the slanted surface.

Another design feature incorporates the needs and space limitations of the family for whom the climber was built, and these features are detailed in each of the climber descriptions. The first three projects are for babies or toddlers; since these are not used for their intended purpose for very long compared to the larger climbers, they also have many other uses.

The last design feature is the strength of the climber. Certain designs can support more weight and withstand more tricks than others. Families that have three thirty-pound-plus children have different needs from those with one thirty-pounder. Multisibling families present another potential problem: sharing a structure. Some handle it better than others; some build two climbers. Read how each climber and the accessories were designed to see if any solutions fit your family's needs and budget.

To add extra strength to all the climbers, there are two optional steps; one or both may be used. The first is to use 2×4 supports and/or 1¼″ dowels to increase the wood bulk of the structure, although this also increases the weight. The other *optional step* is to pin each rung at one or both ends. Drill a small hole for a 1¼×6 screw through the smaller face of the 2×3 into the rung. Countersink the head to protect small fingers; this means you must redrill a wider hole with a ¼″ drill bit to a depth of about ¼″ to recess the head of the screw that you will be inserting. Screw in the 1¼×6 screw. Cover the head with a little wood putty and sand smooth. The photograph shows the step with the rung detached from the frame to demonstrate how the screw will be holding the rung; on your climber, the dowel will already be glued into its socket. (If you are using 2×4 framing, the screw will have to be longer to hold the rung.)

All the climbers are basically two or more ladders attached in some way. Making sure that the rungs are perpendicular to the sides is the best way to ensure success for a ladder and therefore the climbers. They will sit flat on the floor, not slanting to one side or the other.

BABY CLIMBERS

Babies come in all sizes and shapes, and they also come with individual temperaments. One major characteristic of temperament is motor activity; to what degree a baby is active marks a difference among children. Another characteristic is approach/withdrawal, the length of time it takes any young child to warm up to attempting a new activity. Some children are cautious, others are more daring, and still others do not know the meaning of "take it easy." Matching the degree of difficulty of the climber with the degree of motor activity and caution exhibited by any given child is the parents' job when introducing a baby climber.

79

CUSHIONS

The first climber might better be termed a *crawler*. It is designed for seven- to thirteen-month-olds who are looking for the ultimate challenge, to advance over obstacles and gain new heights! If you want to appreciate a baby's challenge, get down on your hands and knees and realize that, proportionally, six inches to the crawler would be sixteen or more inches to the adult.

The cushions are made of 4″ thick urethane foam blocks. They are soft enough to cradle tumbles yet stiff enough to support a baby's weight. The ones pictured are foam blocks 21″ × 21″ × 4″, and they cost about $3.50 apiece. These are covered with old sofa seat covers; yours can easily be wrapped with upholstery fabric just as the exercise mats or soft blocks (see Chapters 8 and 14 for construction details). Combined with a couch, the cushions give a natural place to pull themselves to a standing position. When babies have outgrown this climber's function, the baby cushions miraculously turn into exercise mats or soft blocks!

PLATFORMS

The next baby climber is stiffer, taller, and even more exciting (to a one-year-old). It is designed to bridge the gap from advanced crawl to beginner jump.

The basic units are a 15″ × 24″ × 6″ rectangular platform and a ramp. More ramps and platforms of varying heights can be added if you are so compelled, but two are really all that are necessary. As simplistic as this apparatus may look to an adult, the child views it as a place to practice over and over those skills necessary to negotiate grown-up environments. At first, the climber is an extension of the cushions, providing various levels on which to crawl up and down; in fact, the cushions can be combined with the hard platforms in the crawling stages. Including the ramp adds a new experience of crawling on an inclined/declined surface.

When the child begins to walk (the average age at which children begin to walk is thirteen months), the same experiences are transferred to a new plane. The muscles around the ankle adjust to the change, up or down, in the surface of the ramp. With help, the new walker learns to negotiate where you can oversee and assist.

Another skill that this climber develops most adeptly is that of stepping up and stepping down. Children are drawn to steps, curbs, and blocks by that self-motivating urge to learn how to move around their world, to conquer the skill of ascending and descending stairs so necessary in this civilized wood-and-concrete world. It seems logical to provide a soft and safe place to practice rather than constantly removing toddlers from stairs or leaving them to try steps on concrete porch stoops. Why get into a power struggle with autonomous toddlers whose natural instincts to climb pull them toward the stairs? Blockade the steps and provide an exciting alternative.

Once they have conquered the step, the next goal is the jump. The two-footed jump is quite a feat: the baby has to coordinate balance, raising of the arms, pushing with the thigh muscles, and flexing of the feet and toes, all at the same time and all while suppressing the fear of being totally off the ground. This is one developmental sequence that is easily observable. Parents who appreciate the amount of energy and repetition necessary for a child to attain a skill, whether motor or cognitive, and who appreciate the role of an environment that encourages exploration and practice help children reach their potential.

When this baby climber has fulfilled its purposes for the crawler, walker, stepper, and jumper, it can become an access to sinks, toilets, and light switches, or it can be used as a piece of modular building equipment with other platforms and climbers. It is fun to use the ramp as an incline for balls and trucks although the climber described next is excellent for this, too.

Materials for One Ramp and Platform

- The platforms are made from a 4×4 sheet of ½" plywood; any grade is adequate since it will be covered. Polyurethaning the wood makes it too slippery; the covering hides a multitude of mistakes.
- Nails are used for assembly. Use 1" brads (small-headed nails) or other thin-shafted nails.
- Corner braces inside the platform are four 6" pieces of 2×2, 2×3, or 2×4; for the ramp you need one 14" piece of 2×2, 2×3, or 2×4 (any of these sizes will do).

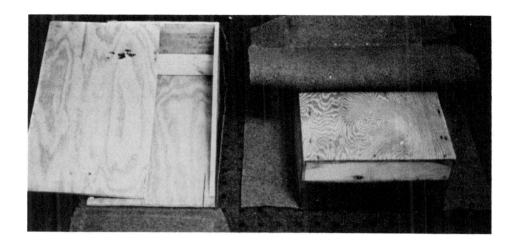

- The covering most recommended is unpadded, nonwoven carpet; it is not too slippery, is nice-looking, easy to cut and to cover; and it costs about $4.50 per square yard. (Sears carries it in its catalogue; very large hardware stores and carpet outlets also usually carry it.) Other coverings might be thin woven carpet or carpet padding covered by heavy fabric.
- Carpet tacks or staples to secure the covering.

Construction for One Ramp and One Platform

1. Draw the following diagram on a 4′ × 4′ piece of ½″ plywood and saw on the lines. The 6″ × 24″ pieces for the sides of the ramp have to be cut on a diagonal. This is not too difficult if there is ample wood to clamp to the workbench; so when sawing, make the first four cuts as indicated in diagram.

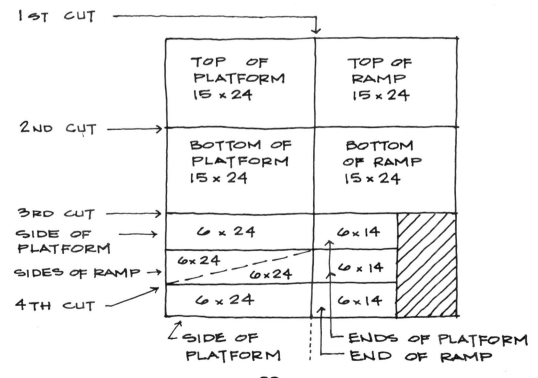

Platform

2A. To assemble the rectangle, glue and nail two of the 6″ braces to the short sides of one of the 6″ × 14″ plywood end pieces. If you have time, use the glue as a clamp by letting it set before nailing. Repeat the process with the other two braces and end piece.

2B. Stand up the end pieces on top of one of the 15″ × 24″ pieces so that, if you could see through the wood, it would look like the diagram below. Again, if you have time, use glue to secure the pieces before fastening. Nail on the large piece, driving four or five brads into the braces and along the edge of the plywood. Repeat the process for the other 15″ × 24″ piece.

2C. Now turn the rectangle on its side and attach the 6″ × 24″ side pieces with glue and nails.

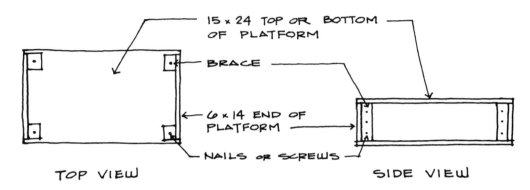

2D TOP VIEW SIDE VIEW

Ramp

3A. To assemble the ramp, attach the 14″ brace to the edge of the 6″ × 14″ piece with glue and nails.

3B. Stand the end piece on top of the 15″ × 24″ bottom piece, centering it along the 15″ side; there will be ½″ on either side. Glue it in place. Drive three or four brads through the bottom and into the brace. (You will have to brace this L-shaped piece of wood so that it is supported when you hammer the nails.)

3C. Attach the side triangles first with glue and then with brads into the brace and along the side edge; then flip it over and drive three or four nails into the bottom and side triangles. If you could see through the wood, it would look like the diagram below.

3D. Attach the top by laying the 15″ × 24″ piece over the side pieces. Center it; it will not be quite flush with either end. Glue and nail the top into the sides.

4. Cover the ramp and rectangle with carpet. Wrap the platforms as you would a present. Use tacks or staples to secure the covering; hammer them in so that there are no protrusions.

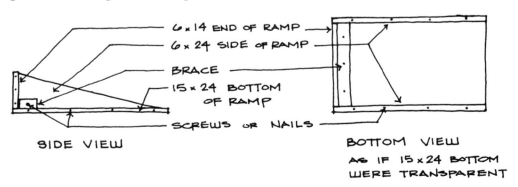

SIDE VIEW

BOTTOM VIEW
AS IF 15 x 24 BOTTOM WERE TRANSPARENT

TODDLER CLIMBER

The toddler climber is for children who are skilled walkers and steppers. It can still be crawled on, but the new dimension is the inclined surface.

The hallmark of eighteen-month-old children is experimentation; they will try almost anything. They find new ways of inserting something into everything or of opening assorted things. They are budding scientists. With the climber, they imagine different ways they can climb up and go down, and then they prove that it can be done. What is the essence of a slide? A lesson in gravity.

The slide has no sides because it is entered from so many different angles and positions; rarely do toddlers climb the ladder to it. It is only 18" off the ground and a full 18" wide to give them plenty of room for maneuvering. If you are nervous about falls, add the exercise mat. The toddler climber is lightweight and portable and can be moved from room to room if Mom or Dad is trying to get some chores finished and Junior wants to tag along. If it is not being used (or used according to the rules), it can easily be folded and stored.

The useful life of this slide for any given toddler is about one year; then, by adding new constructions, these pieces become modulars for the next climber. If you are constructing climbing equipment for a two-year-old and a four-year-old, then the sliding board alone can be constructed and suspended from a low rung on a taller climber and still provide stimulation for both children. The family that already has a store-bought toddler climber can make a sliding board to extend the possibilities for that piece of equipment, too.

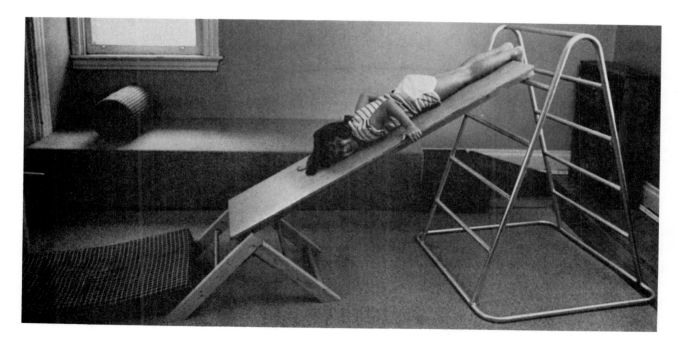

Materials for the Slide

- One ½" thick piece of interior-grade plywood 4' or 5' long and 18" wide forms the sliding surface.
- Anchors are two 1×2s that are 15" long (slightly narrower than the slide).
- You need 1×6 screws to secure the anchors.
- For the optional step of strengthening the slide for heavier children, you need two 5' 2×2s and four carriage bolts, 2" long, and the nuts and washers.

Construction of the Slide

1. Sand all wood and smooth and round the edges.

2. Optional: To strengthen the slide for heavier use, run two 4' or 5' lengths of 2×2 along the underside (about 2" in from each edge). Glue them in place and let them set. Clamp the plywood and 2×2 together and then drill ¼" holes through the slide and 2×2s about 4" from all four ends. On the underside, redrill into the same hole with a ¾" drill bit to a depth of about ¾". (This is countersinking the nuts so that little fingers will not get hurt on the protrusions.) Insert the carriage bolts, heads on the sliding surface, and tap lightly with a hammer until they are flush with the plywood. Put the washers and nuts on the other ends and tighten until they feel snug. This makes the board rigid, and it can then be used as a platform or slide for larger children as well.

3. Attach the anchors to the underside (or to the 2×2s if reinforced) first by gluing them in place along the top and bottom edges. Drill holes for the screws through the anchors and into either the plywood (being careful not to go all the way through it) or the 2×2s. Insert the screws. If you accidentally drill through the plywood, fill the holes with wood putty and sand smooth.

4. Polyurethane generously and let dry. Resand the sliding surface lightly, wipe with a damp cloth, and dry. Add another coat of polyurethane. The more coats of polyurethane, the smoother and more slippery the surface, although two coats are sufficient.

Materials for the Ladder

- Two 2×3s 37″ long are needed for the legs.
- Five 1″ diameter dowels 24″ long make the rungs.
- Two 4″ strap hinges and three ¾″ by 8″ wood screws are the necessary hardware. Ask the hardware person for help if you need it!

Construction of the Ladder

1. Cut two 2×3s 37″ long. Mark a spot on one edge at 21″; place the wood in a miter box or draw on the cut with a protractor and saw at the mark so that the wood has a 45-degree angle. Be sure that the direction of the cut produces one leg 21″ on its *long* side and 18½″ on its short side, as shown in the photo below. Repeat the process with the second 2×3. These four pieces form the legs of the ladder.

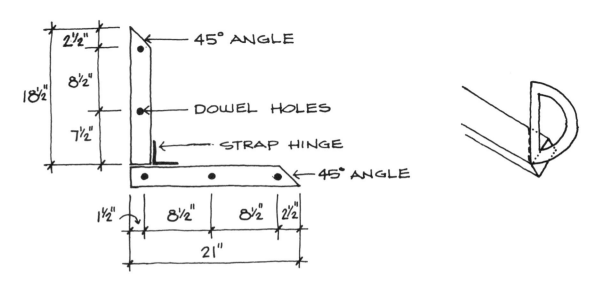

2. Set up the legs as if you were going to assemble the ladder and mark the faces on which you will be drilling. On the longer legs, measuring from the square end, center three spots for drilling at 1½", 10", and 18½". On the shorter legs, center the drilling marks, again from the square end, at 7½" and 16".

3. Drill 1" diameter holes ½" deep at each of the marks on all four legs.

4. Glue the dowels into the 2×3s to form two ladders. Square the ladders using a square (tool), book, or shirt cardboard so that the rungs are perpendicular to the ladder legs. (See the climber introduction section for details if you are unsure of this step.) Let the glue set. If you have pipe clamps, use them.

5. Laying the three-rung ladder with the inside face up, position the shorter ladder at a 90-degree angle to attach it to the hinges. Be sure that, when the ladder is closed, the inside faces will be together. Position the 4" strap hinges and mark the drill holes. Take the ladder apart and drill each hole to the depth of the screws you are using.

6. Attach the strap hinges to the longer ladder first and then reassemble the second ladder and drive in the screws.

7. Sand all rough spots and edges; polyurethane the wood.

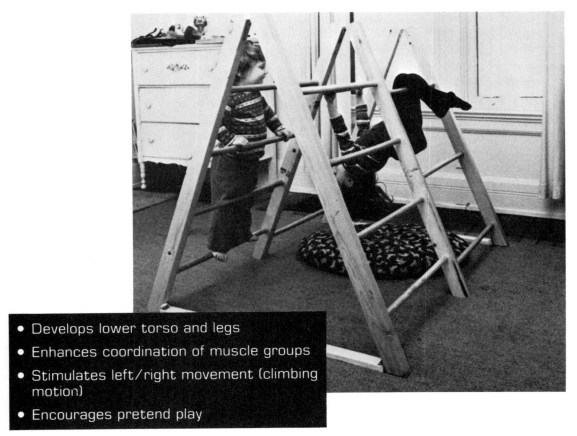

- Develops lower torso and legs
- Enhances coordination of muscle groups
- Stimulates left/right movement (climbing motion)
- Encourages pretend play

A-FRAME CLIMBERS

This series of climbers is recommended especially for younger children because the climbers have slanted ladders to put the climbing load on the legs rather than the upper torso. For the under-four age group, the thigh muscles are much more capable of bearing the body's weight for a longer period of time. If you are building for two children, one of whom is younger, then the A-frames are a better choice than the box climbers described later in this chapter. They are all

under four feet in height, are strong enough to support a couple of preschoolers, are very hard to tip over, and offer many variations as a climber and as a tent frame. They fold up for easy storage or for setup outside.

Children seem to be ready for the A-frame at around two and a half or three years. Mom or Dad build it and then watch their firstborn child do wonderful tricks. Sometime later, a secondborn child begins to pull herself up on the climber. This scenario has taken place in a number of families that have experimented with this book's equipment. The parents found it was time to make some decisions about the climber. One family put it in the older child's bedroom and made it off-limits to the younger. Two families added an extra-large exercise mat under the climber and let the younger child climb. Another family brought it out from storage only when it could be parent-supervised, allowing the younger child to experiment on the A-frame. The adults made conscious decisions about their toddlers' use of the large-muscle equipment.

All the A-frames have fixed-pin strap hinges that hold the two ladders together at the top. A strap hinge is a long triangular hinge as compared to a door hinge, which has rectangular plates; each attaches to a different-shaped surface and bears weight differently. The pins on hinges have two names: *fixed pin* and *loose pin*. A loose pin hinge allows the two plates to be separated when the pin is pulled.

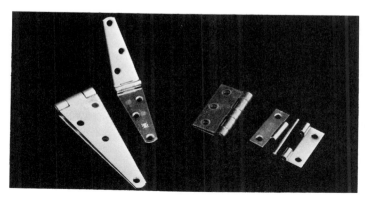

- Develops lower torso and legs
- Enhances coordination of muscle groups
- Stimulates left/right movement (climbing motion)
- Encourages pretend play

THOMAS'S CLIMBER

This is the simplest climber to build, and it is very portable. With or without platforms and slides, Thomas's climber offers children hours of fun. It measures three feet by three feet and therefore is very economical of space. And it only costs about $14 to make.

The climber design serves a family with four children from age twenty months through seven years. Mom built it in a little over three hours spread over two days (to let the glue dry). It has a removable platform that fits over the two top rungs. The children climb, pretend, and even draw on it. The climber sits atop a futon to cushion any possible falls.

This design needs to be placed on a mat or rug because it is more prone to sliding than the A-frame climbers that have wood supports between the legs. The cord strung between the legs keeps it from sliding open but doesn't prevent it from closing up. It is advisable to cover the cords with a mat to keep children from tripping on them.

If you are considering a climber that is to be used inside and outside, this is a good choice as it is so portable. Making two of them, modifying the rungs to be only 24 inches wide instead of 36, and making lots of slides and platforms could make this climber as versatile as Moomaw's Two-Towered Climber (described later).

Materials

- The sides are four 4' 2×3s.
- The climber as pictured requires eight 1" diameter dowels 36" long.
- The necessary hardware items are two 4" strap hinges and the ¾" screws to hold them in place. Ask the hardware person to fit the screws if you need help!
- Four strong eyelets hold the heavy cord or rope (about 4' long) at the bases.
- The platform across the top is made from ½" or ¾" plywood or pine board. It is about 12" wide by about 34" long; sizes will vary with each climber.

Construction

1. Cut and sand the side pieces and the dowels.

2. Mark four ends of the 2×3s as the *bottom* of the climber. Measuring from the bottom, center the marks for the drill holes at 8", 18", 28", and 38" on each of the legs as shown below.

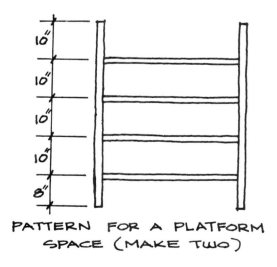

PATTERN FOR A PLATFORM
SPACE (MAKE TWO)

3. Drill 1" diameter holes at each mark at least ½" deep.

4. Assemble each half of the climber to make two ladders. Use ample amounts of wood glue in one leg. Insert the dowels; if the fit is tight, tap them in place with a hammer. Use a piece of wood between the hammer face and the dowel to prevent damage to the rung. Put glue in the holes of the opposite leg and assemble the ladder. Tap the dowels in place, if necessary. Square the ladder, so that the sides are perpendicular to the rungs, with a square (tool) or a shirt cardboard or book. Use pipe clamps if you have them while the glue sets (at least four hours). Wipe off any excess glue.

5. Lay out the two halves of the ladder, tops together. Center the strap hinges on the 2×3s with the pin directly over the space between the tops. Mark the spots for the screws. Make sure that the hinges are placed so that the climber will close.

6. Remove the hinges and drill the holes. (Remember, if some of this is confusing to you, there is an explanation of how to use each tool in Chapter 6.) Reassemble the hinges and insert the screws.

7. Stand up the climber and determine the slant that you want. Drill small holes at the base of each leg and insert the eyelets. Tie pieces of rope or heavy cord between the eyelets of opposite legs to keep the climber from opening as the children climb.

8. Optional: Pin the dowels in place as directed in the climber introduction section.

9. To make the platform, measure from the outside of one top rung to the outside of the other. Add about 1″ to your mea-

surement to determine how wide to make the platform. Too much overhang is dangerous because it will cause the platform to flip up when the child puts pressure on the edge. The length can vary according to your desires. The platform pictured is 34″ long; it is a 1×12 pine board.

10. Lay the wood over the rungs and position the anchors from underneath on the *inside* of the dowels. Mark where they go with a pencil.

11. Remove the platform and glue on the anchors with ample amounts of wood glue. Let it set.

12. *Optional:* Polyurethane the climber and platform. Also, the platform can be covered with nonwoven carpeting or heavy fabric for a softer surface.

- Develops lower torso and legs
- Enhances coordination of muscle groups
- Stimulates left/right movement (climbing motion)
- Encourages pretend play

McCUSKER'S CLIMBER

This climber first served a 2½-year-old whose family rented an apartment in a two-family house. They had access to a yard but could not put up any permanent play equipment. Mom wanted a portable climber, slanted sides, and a variety of rung configurations without building two different frames.

She built this climber, which is one of the simplest to construct, for about $25; it is a very strong construction and takes up a space measuring only three by four feet. It provides climbing, sliding, sitting, and hanging places as well as playhouse space when covered. It can have a platform space at the top as described in Thomas's A-frame Climber. It also is very portable, folding flat when the loose pins are pulled on the hinges at the bases.

This climber now has a home in Florida, and the family has two children using it.

Materials

- The side and center supports are made from six 4' lengths of 2×3s, sanded smooth.
- Rungs are 2' long, 1" diameter dowels; there are thirteen in this design.
- The base is two lengths of 1×2 about 3' or 4' long each, depending on the degree of slant you want in the climber.
- Hardware includes three 4" strap hinges and four 1½ loose pin hinges. On loose-pin (as opposed to fixed-pin) hinges the pin can be pulled out to separate the two plates.
- Also, you will need sixteen ¾×8 or ¾×10 screws for the trap hinges. The loose-pin hinges usually come with ½" screws.

Construction

1. Label each face A, B, C, or D, as shown in the diagram; the center has two faces, B and C. Also, mark the tops with an **X** or another symbol. Drill 1" diameter holes ½" into the 2×3s at intervals specified in the drawing below. Do all measuring from the *bottom* so that your rungs are at the same height on both sides.

5. If you have decided to skip step 4, sand down all the edges of each leg so that they are not sharp.

6. Lay out the ladders on a floor with tops together. Be sure A and B are opposite one another. Line up the three strap hinges (sides facing up to allow the hinge to close completely.) Mark the wood for the screw holes.

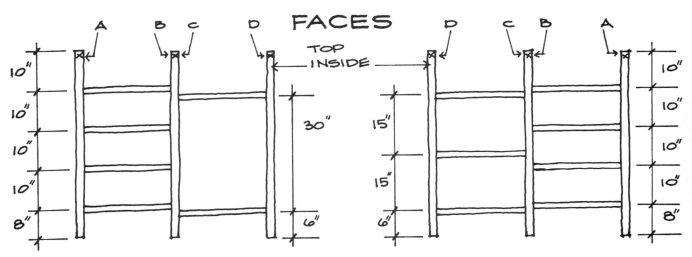

FACES

A   B C   D   TOP —INSIDE—   D   C B   A

10" 10" 10" 10" 8"   30"   6"   15" 15" 6"   10" 10" 10" 10" 8"

2. Assemble faces A and B into a ladder by gluing dowels into sockets, using generous amounts of wood glue. Wipe off the excess. If the fit is tight (and that is a benefit), tap the dowels in place by putting the ladder on its side; use an extra piece of wood between the hammer and climber surface so as not to damage the wood. Make sure the rungs are squared at a 90-degree angle to the sides using a square, a piece of cardboard, or a book corner. Let the glue set. Use a pipe clamp if available.

3. After the glue has hardened, assemble faces and C and D. Let the glue set again.

4. Optional: In order for the climber to sit flat on the floor, each tip must be leveled. With someone holding up the sides as if they were already attached, set up the climber on a hard, flat surface. Lay a piece of wood or a wide ruler on the floor next to each leg; mark a line on the side of each foot parallel to the floor. Saw off the ends at each line.

Cinti., O.   513-681-4409

7. Remove the hinges and drill the holes. Reset the hinges and secure the screws.

8. Now set up the climber in an A-frame position (reminding the children that it is not yet finished). Put the connecting base-boards (about 3'–5' long, depending on the degree of slant you want) between the end legs. Line up the loose-pin hinges and mark the holes. Remove them and drill. Now remove the pins from each hinge and attach the appropriate half of the hinge to the leg or base. Realign and insert the pins.

9. Sand down all all top corners and polyurethane the climber.

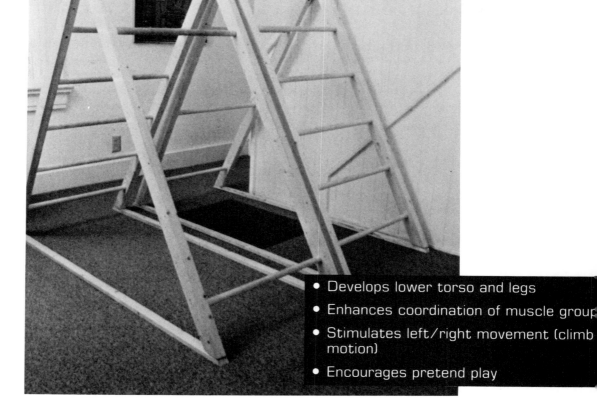

- Develops lower torso and legs
- Enhances coordination of muscle group
- Stimulates left/right movement (climb motion)
- Encourages pretend play

PACHAN'S CLIMBER

This family was expecting another member when the climber was designed. They wanted a slanted ladder because the daughter was just three, and they expected to use the climber for the new baby as well. They wanted a very portable model so that Mom could carry it outside on warm days. The room in which they planned to put the climber also served as their drawing and sewing room, so the climber could not have too large a base. Finally, they wanted a climber that could also serve as a playhouse to stimulate pretending.

They built two structures for their children but found that one was all they used for their needs at the time. Their little girl found plenty of challenge in one, and the indoor space was a little cramped using two climbers. Outdoors, they use two climbers with lots of accessories. They spent about $20 for one A-frame.

Materials for One A-frame

- Sides are four 5' lengths of 2×3s.
- Rungs are 1" dowels cut 2' long. If you are making one frame, try five rungs on one side and three on the other. Also, for the base you will need four pieces of doweling 1¼" long.
- Each base is approximately a 5½' length of 1×2; these pieces should not be precut because they should be sized after the climber is built. You will need two of them.
- Two 4–5" strap hinges hold the points together.

Construction

1. Lay one set of the 5′ 2×3s on the floor at the angle that you will want the top to be (between 45 and 60 degrees), overlapping the boards. Scribe a line (AB) on the lower board and mark point (C) on the bottom 2×3. Saw on line AB.

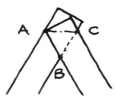

2. Lay the board that you just sawed onto one of the other 2×3s. Using the edge that you just cut, draw a line on the new 2×3 to get the same angle for the other set of legs. Saw along this line.

3. Optional: In order to flatten out the top of the climber, draw a line across the 2×3s from A to C on the other two boards and saw.

4. You will be making a choice of the rung variations that you want on your climber. Choose a five-rung ladder (to accommodate a platform) or a six-rung ladder (to accommodate a single top rung) for the longer leg side; and choose a two- or three-rung ladder (to accommodate hanging and flipping) for the other side. You also might choose to repeat the five-rung pattern on this shorter leg. Set up the bases of the climber as if they had rungs already in place. Mark the surfaces that you will be drilling; measuring from the bottom, place a mark starting at 6″ and thereafter at the inch marks for the rung pattern you have chosen. Drill the holes for the dowels, 1″ in diameter to a depth of ½″.

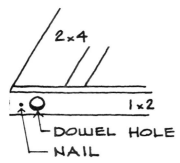

5. Assemble each ladder separately by putting ample amounts of wood glue into the holes and inserting the dowels. If there is a tight fit, gently tap the dowels in place, putting an extra piece of wood between the hammer and climber. Square the ladders with a square, book, or shirt cardboard, and let the glue set. If you have pipe clamps, use them.

6. With someone else holding the ladders together as if the strap hinges were in place, place a board or ruler along the floor next to each leg as pictured and draw a line. Saw off the excess at the line to make the climber sit flat on the floor.

7. To attach the strap hinges, set up the ladders and position the hinges, marking the drill holes. Take the ladders apart and drill holes to the depth of the screws. Attach one side of the hinges to one ladder. Reposition the other ladder and drive in the remaining screws. Do not let the children climb yet; it will bend the hinges!

8. To attach the base, lay the climber on its side. Cut 1×2s to fit from the *outside* of one leg to the *outside* of the other. Using brads or small nails, nail the base to the legs to hold them temporarily in place. Drill 1" diameter holes through the 1×2s and into each leg to a depth of ½". As you pull out the nails, mark each leg and base as faces A, B, C, and D so that each time you move the climber you can reassemble it with ease. Put ample amounts of wood glue into the holes in the base pieces and insert the 1¼" long dowels. If there is a tight fit, gently tap the dowels in place. Let the glue set.

9. Sand rough points, edges, and wood until smooth, then polyurethane.

LONGER LEGS

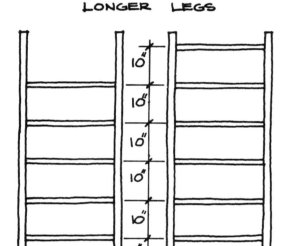

PATTERN FOR A PLATFORM SPACE

PATTERN FOR A SINGLE TOP RUNG

SHORTER LEGS

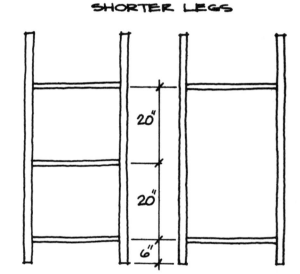

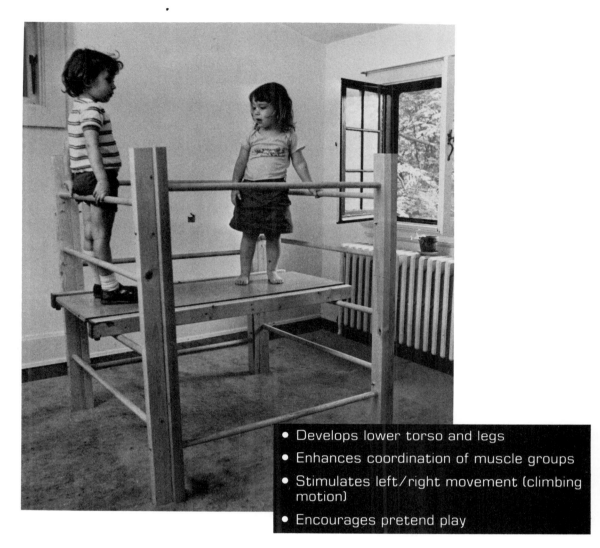

- Develops lower torso and legs
- Enhances coordination of muscle groups
- Stimulates left/right movement (climbing motion)
- Encourages pretend play

BOX CLIMBERS

These climbers are especially easy to construct, but they are less portable than the A-frame models. Also, the box climbers have a four-foot vertical ladder and, therefore, are more suited to an older child (at least three years old) who has the upper body strength and balance to use it safely. Another safety measure, especially when the climber is introduced to the child for the first weeks, is the addition of the exercise mat.

Box climbers do offer a variety of activities when you add platforms or use covers. It is easy to imagine that they are forts, rockets, houses, etc., with an upstairs and a downstairs.

A vertical climber needs a wide base if it is to be used by heavy children because their weight could pull it over on top of them. Adding extra width to the bottom with boards or triangles will prevent the climber from tipping. Both Alber's and Moomaw's climbers have descriptions of two different base extensions. An optional step to add strength to the climber is described in the climber introduction section; it is pinning each rung at one or both ends with a small screw. When the climber is going to serve more than one child in a household, this step is recommended, especially for the box climbers, as they will be stressed from four sides.

- Develops lower torso and legs
- Enhances coordination of muscle groups
- Stimulates left/right movement (climbing motion)
- Encourages pretend play

ALBERS'S CLIMBER

This climber is a box shape 22 by 36 inches and 4 feet high. It was built for a three-year-old who kept it in her room at her first residence, which was an apartment. When the family moved, she put it on the enclosed porch of her new house. At present there is a sister who is toddling up to the climber (the slide is on the lowest rung) and another child who will be using it in about a year.

It is a small climber but easily accommodates lots of motor and imaginary activity with its accessories, which are described in the climber accessories section. One feature of this climber and of Runyan's Climber (detailed later in this chapter) is the steel pipe rungs. The father of the little girl who owned it worked at a machine shop and had access to the pipe, a press, and a drill. He took advantage of his occupation to provide raw material for building the climbers. The rungs add extra weight as well as strength to the structures. Albers's and Runyan's climbers can also be built with wood dowels; the construction section outlines this procedure because wood dowels are more readily available as construction materials than the metal pipe. It will be the same dimensions as the climber pictured.

Another feature of this climber is its size; having a small width and a vertical ladder, this climber could tip over when a heavier child uses it. Two base pieces to give it stability are included in the construction section. It is small and light enough to be carried around by two adults, but it does not fold up, so it has to have a permanent spot in the household. It costs about $18 to construct.

Materials

- Four 2×3 posts are the sides; they are 4' high.
- There are thirteen rungs—five 32" rungs and eight 22" rungs—made of 1" dowels.
- Bases are 1×3s cut 18" longer than the short rungs, in this case 40". (The base pieces are longer to give the climber stability. The climber pictured used to have longer bases, but the extending pieces were cut off—instead of unscrewed—when the climber was moved to its new home.)
- Four 1¼×6 wood screws secure the bases.

Construction

1. Cut all wood and sand smooth; round the corners.

2. Set up the side pieces and mark them as faces A, B, C, and D; each corner 2×3 will have two faces. Measuring from the *bottom* so that your rungs will be even, mark the spots for the rungs according to the diagram below or according to your own design. (If you make up a pattern, do not put rungs on adjacent sides at the same height. Offset them slightly so that your drill holes are not too close. Opposite-side rungs should be at the same height to accommodate platforms.)

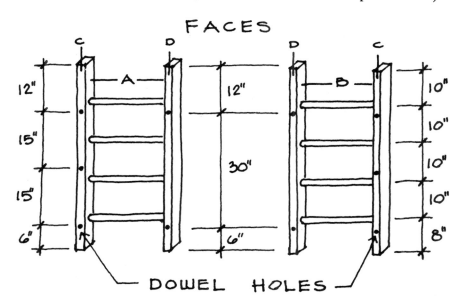

3. Drill all 1″ diameter holes ½″ deep into the side pieces.

4. Assemble two opposite faces, the ones with the most rungs, as you would two ladders. Use ample amounts of wood glue in the holes; insert the dowels or tap them in if the fit is tight. (Use an extra piece of wood between the face of the wood and the hammer so as not to damage your surfaces.) Wipe off the excess glue. Make sure the rungs are squared at a 90-degree angle to the sides and let the glue set. Use pipe clamps if you have them.

5. Assemble the remaining faces, following the directions in Step 4. Set up the climber between the wall and a table, square the newly inserted rungs, and let the glue set. If you have pipe clamps available, use them while the glue sets.

6. Turn the climber onto its top and lay the bases across the smaller width. Drill appropriate-diameter holes through the bases and into the legs of the climber. Screw in the wood screws until they are flush with the surfaces.

7. Optional: Pin the rungs as described in the climber introduction section.

8. Sand any rough points and polyurethane.

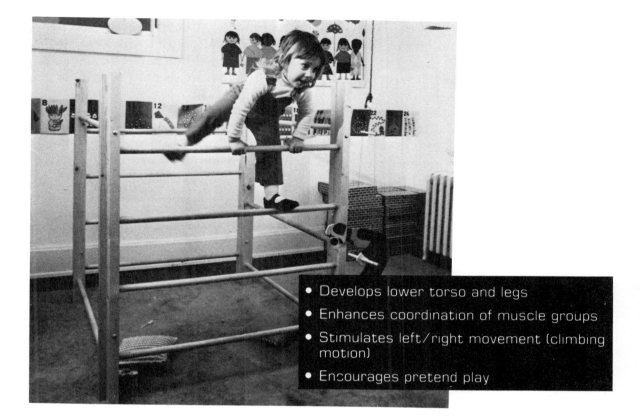

- Develops lower torso and legs
- Enhances coordination of muscle groups
- Stimulates left/right movement (climbing motion)
- Encourages pretend play

AGNA'S CLIMBER

This three-by-three-foot climber was built for one three-year-old. It had a permanent location in her room. It has successfully moved to its third location in as many states. Mom built the climber for its options with the accessories; the slide doubles as a large platform at various heights off the ground. It can be used as a climber or as a prop for house play and is described in the accessories section. By the way, these pictures were taken after the climber had been in use for a long time, so no mat is shown; however, *an exercise mat under the climber is always advisable for beginners.*

Although the climber can be disassembled, it is not a design you might move indoors and outdoors daily. It is secured with eight carriage bolts, two through

each corner of the frame; another simple way it can be assembled is by using two 2" loose-pin hinges (doors are attached to a frame this way) in each of the four corners so that it can be disassembled more quickly. The construction section details both assembly directions so that you can choose which one is best for your household.

This climber design offers its owner lots of rung variations on its four-foot-high faces and different heights for platforms and accessories. If you choose this design for one or more fifty-pound child, it is recommended that you use 1¼" dowels or design each face with three support beams instead of two as in McCusker's A-Frame Climber.

Materials

- Sides are eight 4' lengths of 2×3s.
- The sides have a total of thirteen 1" (or 1¼") dowels in 3' lengths.
- The climber is attached with either eight 4" carriage bolts or eight 2" loose-pin hinges and screws.

Construction

1. Cut all wood and sand smooth, rounding all top corners.

2. Drill 1" diameter holes ½" into the 2×3s at intervals specified in the diagram.

Mark the tops with an *X* or another symbol. Do *all* measuring from the opposite or *bottom* end so that your rungs are the same height.

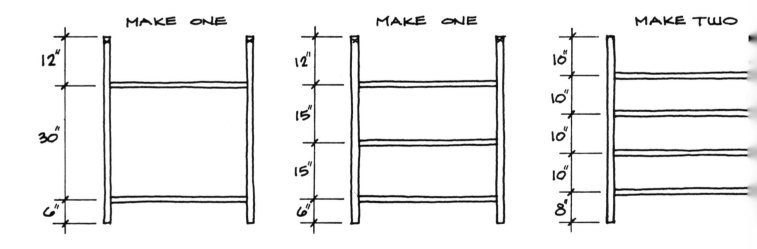

3. Assemble each of the four ladders by gluing dowels into the sockets, using generous amounts of wood glue. Wipe off the excess. If the fit is tight (and that is a benefit), tap the dowels in place by putting an extra piece of wood between the hammer and the surface so as not to damage it. Make sure the rungs are at a 90-

degree angle to the sides, using a piece of cardboard or a book corner. Let the glue set. Use pipe clamps if they are available.

4. Deciding on a method to attach the sides, follow either step 4A or step 4B. The second method is harder to accomplish but makes the climber more portable.

4A. With someone holding ladder A and ladder B at a 90-degree angle, drill an appropriate-diameter hole (usually ¼″) through both 2×3s about 14″ from the top; drill into the 2″ (really 1½″) thickness of the 2×3 first, then into the other 2×3 as deep as the drill permits. Remove the first

board. Use this partially drilled hole as the guide for drilling the rest of the way through. Insert the carriage bolt to maintain the alignment. Drill the second hole about 14″ from the bottom. Repeat the process until all eight bolts are in place. Next, removing one bolt at a time, redrill eight 1″ diameter holes about ¾″ deep into one end of each of the holes you just drilled; this will recess the nut end so that children will not catch skin or fingers on a protrusion. Tap in the carriage bolts, and secure the nuts just until tight.

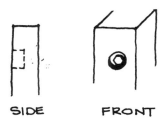

SIDE   FRONT

4B. With someone holding ladder A and ladder B at a 90-degree angle, mark the holes for two hinges. Hinges should be positioned about 14″ from top and bottom

with pins directly over the seams. (Make sure the hinge will close flat.) Remove the hinges and drill the holes. Realign the hinges and secure them with the screws. Now line up the other face A opposite its mate and next to B. Repeat the hinging process. Attach the remaining ladder C to close the box in the same manner. To move the climber about, pull out two sets of pins at opposite corners; fold the attached ladders together.

5. Optional: Pin the rungs as described in the climber introduction section.

6. Sand all top edges and corners; polyurethane.

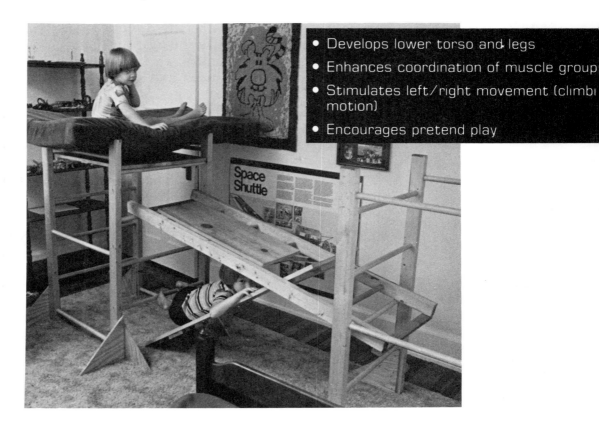

- Develops lower torso and legs
- Enhances coordination of muscle group
- Stimulates left/right movement (climbi motion)
- Encourages pretend play

MOOMAW'S CLIMBER

The family for whom this climber was designed has two children, ages four and six. They were very adept in gross motor control and wanted a climber that would offer a large number of variations and would still be strong and stable. Because two children would be the owners, the parents decided that two towers with connecting structures suited their needs. The climber would be kept indoors, so it did not need to be very portable (or so Mom thought).

Each of the two vertical ladder climbers, born out of the Moomaws' needs, is two by two feet square and four feet high, with triangular plywood stabilizers at

the bases. The climber started its life in the basement (with the exercise mats), but Mom found it was not used as often as she liked. Then it was moved to the children's bedroom, and again Mom was not satisfied that it was being used often enough. It was then moved to the dining room (a central room in this five-room house), where it was used quite often. But the children had another passion that shared time with climbing, and that was artwork. They would carry down from the desk in their bedroom quantities of paper, tape, paper towel rolls, string, etc., to construct projects near where the adults worked. So Mom again changed the environment. This time the climber went back to their bedroom, and the desk came down to the dining room. (The dining room table was in the kitchen.) The children, one and a half years older at this point, played in their room more often, especially when friends came to play, and the desk provided a place for quiet, concentrated work in the downstairs area.

The boys pretend a great deal, using the climber as a basic prop. It has become a huge variety of things, from a spaceship to a castle, and they do tricks that range from balancing stunts to hanging upside down. Since their climbers have so many accessories, they can design a whole space to fit the feat or fantasy that they have in mind. Their space, between the beds or at the ends of them, is not large, but it is well used.

The two towers and all the accessories cost about $45 and took about eighteen hours of manpower (actually womanpower, because Mom built the whole thing). She constructed it over two months of work in a toy group that met once a week.

Materials for One Tower

- The frame of each climber is made up of four 4' lengths of 2×3.
- There are thirteen 1" diameter dowels cut in 24" lengths in each tower.
- Eight 8"×10" triangular pieces of ⅜" plywood are used to stabilize each climber. Mark a piece of plywood as shown below.

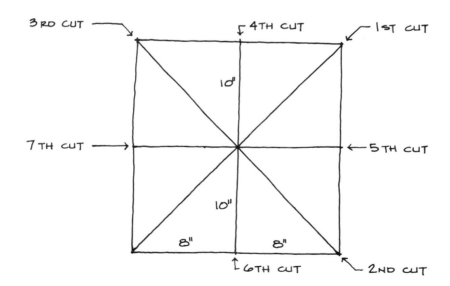

- Sixteen 1×6 screws secure the bases for one tower.
- Wood glue and (optional) thirteen 1¼"×6" screws secure the rungs.

Construction

1. Cut the plywood as shown in the diagram above and sand all wood; remove any sharp corners with sandpaper or rasp.

2. Set up the four corner 2×3s and mark faces A, B, C, and D; each piece will have two faces. Measuring from the *bottom* so that your rungs will be even, mark the spots for the rungs according to the diagram below or according to your own design. (If you make up a pattern, do not put rungs on adjacent sides at the same height. Offset them slightly so that your drill holes are not too close.)

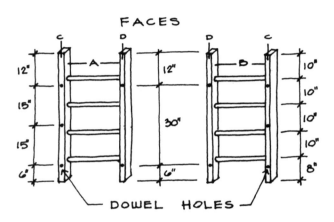

FACES

DOWEL HOLES

3. Drill all 1″ diameter holes ½″ deep into the side pieces.

4. Assemble two opposite faces, the ones with the most rungs, as you would two ladders. Use ample amounts of wood glue in the holes; insert the dowels or tap them in if the fit is tight. (Use an extra piece of wood between the face of the wood and the hammer so as not to damage your surfaces.) Wipe off the excess glue. Make sure the rungs are squared at a 90-degree angle to the sides and let the glue set. Use pipe clamps if you have them.

5. Assemble the remaining faces following the same directions. Set the climber up between the wall and a table, square the newly inserted rungs, and let the glue set. If you have pipe clamps available, use them to set the glue.

6. Optional: To add strength to the climber, pin each rung at one or both ends as described in the climber introduction.

7. The climber is ready to have the base triangles attached, but they add extra inches to the width, so drill the holes but do not attach them because you will have a great deal of difficulty getting the climber through a door to the place where you will be setting it up! To drill the holes, take one triangle and place it against the climber leg; use a clamp to hold it in place while you drill. After you have drilled two holes through the triangle and into the climber, label the triangle face and leg face that touch one another as 1A. As you drill the remaining stabilizers, mark each leg and triangle as you finish 2A, 3A, and so on through 8A. (When you make a second tower, mark them 1B, 2B, and so one through 8B.) This will prevent you from having to search later for the holes that match each leg.

8. Sand any rough or sharp edges and polyurethane the wood.

9. Set up the climber in the desired space and screw in the bases. (To move around the house through standard-width doors, remove only four of the triangles.)

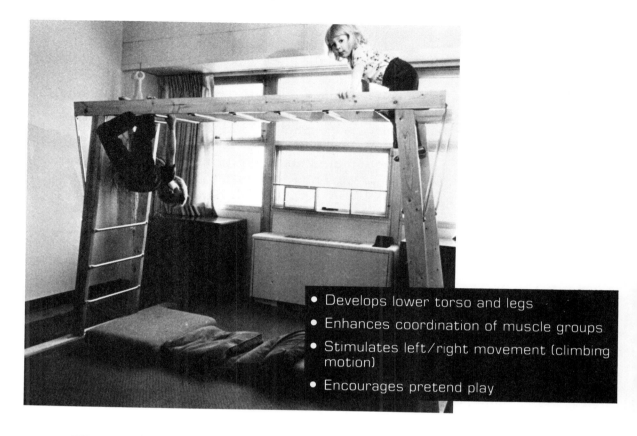

- Develops lower torso and legs
- Enhances coordination of muscle groups
- Stimulates left/right movement (climbing motion)
- Encourages pretend play

RUNYAN'S CLIMBER

This family wanted an indoor climber for its four- and six-year-olds. They lived in a two-bedroom apartment on the ninth floor of a high-rise and needed a large-muscle outlet close at hand. Since the children were older and could safely play on a taller climber, the parents decided on a single five-foot-high structure that took up about 21 square feet of their bedroom, which had 132 square feet.

The climber offered the children space to climb, hang, slide, relax, jump, and pretend. They both learned to move hand over hand across the horizontal ladder quite quickly. The sliding board laid across the top rungs gave the children a platform for reading.

Although not a highly portable climber, it does disassemble into three pieces; when the family went home to Grandma and Grandpa's for the summer, the

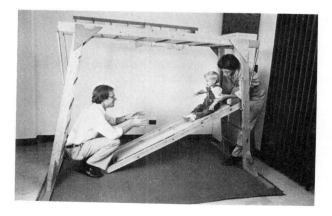

family lent it to another family, who put it up in their basement. When the Runyans returned, they reassembled the climber, this time in the alcove behind the living room couch. Since the baby was out of the crib, the children's bedroom became the sleeping room, and the alcove became the apartment's play area. The shelves and toys were installed along the wall. The youngest child, now eighteen months old, began his conquest of the climber under more supervision.

This climber, as pictured, is made from the 22-inch metal rungs custom-made in a machine shop by Albers' dad, but it can also be constructed easily with dowels. The construction directions call for dowels since these are more readily available than metal pipes. The Runyans also added four rungs as "handles." In the construction with wood dowels, these handles are unnecessary. The climber costs approximately $45 to make.

Materials

- The overhead ladder is made from two 7′ lengths of 2×4s; the side ladders are four 5′ lengths of 2×4. Carefully select 2×4s that are not warped or twisted.
- There are fifteen 24″ rungs made from 1″ diameter doweling.
- The bases are two 5′ lengths of 1×4.
- The stabilizers at the top are four ⅜″ thick plywood triangles, 10″ × 10″ on two of the sides.
- The stabilizers at the bottom are four 9″ × 9″ triangles cut from a 2×10 pine board. (Remember, most lumberyards can cut to specifications one or several pieces of wood called for in this design, especially the thicker triangles.)
- Twelve 2½″ angle braces position the structures.
- Twenty 1×8 round-head screws secure the top triangles; forty-eight ½×6 flat-head screws secure the angle braces. The 2×10 triangles are secured with eight 2½×8 flat-head screws.

Construction

1. Construct the three ladders according to the diagram below. Drill 1″ diameter holes ½″ into the 2×4s at the specified intervals.

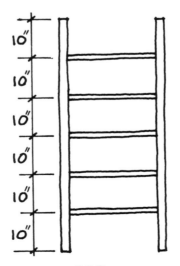

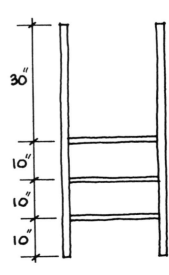

2. Assemble the ladders by gluing the dowels into the sockets, using generous amounts of wood glue. If the fit is tight (and this is a benefit), tap the dowels in place by putting the ladder on its side; use an extra piece of wood between the hammer and climber surface so as not to damage the climber or dowel. Make sure the rungs are at a 90-degree angle to the sides, using a square, book, or shirt cardboard. Let the glue set. If you have pipe clamps, use them while the glue is drying.

3. Optional: In the climber pictured, the legs are placed at an angle to the horizontal ladder to increase the width of the base. If you want to include this step, cut off about 8 degrees of wood, using a protractor to draw the lines at each end, or use a miter box that has a 9-degree setting. Be careful to match the ends of the same ladder and reverse the angle from one ladder to the other. Cut off a whole inch; it's easier than cutting into a corner.

4. At this point, sand and polyurethane all the wood because assembly should be done where the climber is to be stationed in your home.

5. Optional: Pin the rungs for added strength as directed in the climber introduction section.

6. To begin assembly of the climber, attach the angle braces to the tops of each vertical ladder. (If the legs are cut at an angle, bend the angles by clamping them to the workbench and tapping them with a hammer until they will accept the top ladder.)

Center each vertical ladder on the 5' 1×4s and mark the holes for the angle braces on the inside of the ladder. Drill the holes and attach the legs and base. Now position the 2×10 triangles. With someone else holding them in place, drill holes through the leg into the triangle to the length of your 2½" screws. Lubricate your screw threads with a little wood glue and screw them in. Repeat the process from the bottom of the 1×4s.

7. With one person holding each leg, place the horizontal ladder above the legs (about 6" from each end) and mark the holes in the angles for drilling. Lay the ladder down and drill the holes. Reposition the ladder and secure the top to the legs.

8. Now position each of the four plywood triangles, clamping each as you drill the holes, and screw them in place. Your climber is now in its permanent home!

9. To disassemble the climber into three pieces, remove the two screws through the plywood triangles into the legs and the screws through the angle braces into each leg.

- Develops lower torso and legs
- Enhances coordination of muscle groups
- Stimulates left/right movement (climbing motion)
- Encourages pretend play

HOPPERT'S AND CASSINELLI'S STORE-BOUGHT CLIMBERS

All the other climbers in the book are homemade; these are purchased equipment. They are included in the book for purposes of both comparison and choice. They are expensive compared to the homemade versions, but they are readily available to those who do not want or feel unable to make a climber. The wooden box climber costs about $260, and one aluminum A-frame costs about $90, both exclusive of shipping charges.

The box climber was purchased by a mom who wanted a strong, variable climber with lots of pretend play value that she did not have to build. It is portable in the sense that it can easily be disassembled; however, because it is made of hardwood instead of pine, it is very heavy. When the climber was purchased, the family had three children; the fifth will start enjoying it in about four months, so it has about five or six more years of service yet to give.

The A-frame climber belongs to the author and was bought one year before this book was even conceived. At present it is in its fifth year of use. Since it is made of aluminum, it is very light and the children can manipulate it with ease; but it is a one-piece construction and cannot be folded up and put away. Also, the door frames of the house must be at least 40" wide in order to carry the climber in and out of the house or from room to room.

Community Playthings, Route 213, Rifton, NY 12471 (914-658-3141) makes these and other climbers as well as school equipment for institutional and home use. The company also carries quality special-education equipment for those who might need it. To locate other companies that make similar products, check the

Yellow Pages for local school supply companies. Those of you in small towns can send for catalogues by getting addresses from suppliers in big cities (volume sellers) from the phone books in the local library.

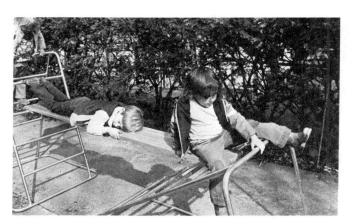

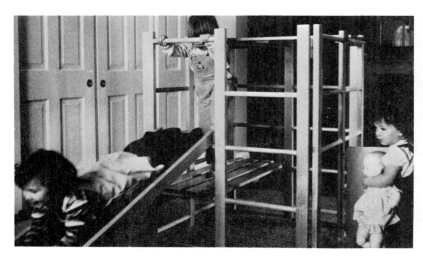

CLIMBER ACCESSORIES

The climber becomes a huge manipulative toy when you add one or more of the following accessories. The child creates new spaces just by moving one board. Each accessory is designed to be as light as possible for the weight it must hold so that the children can do their own moving. The ladder, platforms, and slides described are meant to be interchangeable pieces and have a number of functions so that, in a small home or apartment, a few accessories offer many possibilities.

All the accessories attach to the climber rungs in basically the same way. To keep the platform or slide from sliding off, 1×2s (or 2×2s, if that is what is left over in your wood pile) are secured to the underside of the platform or slide to fit on one or both sides of a rung.

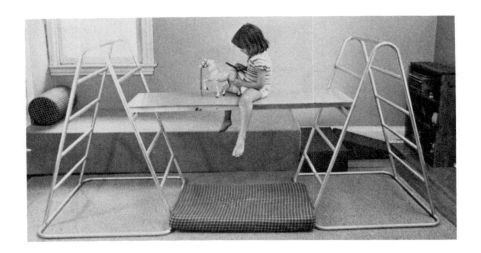

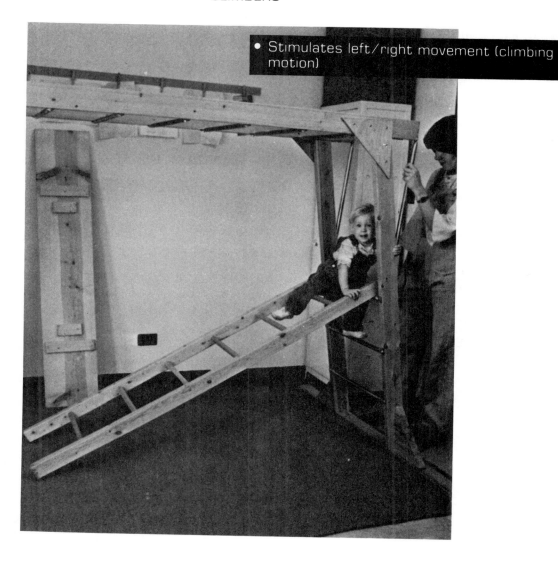

Stimulates left/right movement (climbing motion)

LADDER

A ladder between two climbers or leading on an incline up to one is a daring piece of equipment; it encourages eye-hand or eye-foot coordination with each rung. It has great pretend value, and, because the ladder is lightweight, it can be maneuvered by the children according to their fanciful needs and desires. The ladder can be used by itself or as the base for a platform or slide; its uses, the size of your space, and the width of your climber determine its length and width. For extra strength, the dowels can be pinned through the 2×3s as directed in the climber introduction section.

Materials

- Two 2×3s form the sides, and 1" dowels are the rungs. The ladder should be between 3½' and 6' in length, between 16" and 24" in width, and the rungs spaced 8", 9", or 10" apart.
    To determine size, take into account the width of the sliding board, your climber, and any other equipment that will be used with the ladder. Measure the interior width of your climber and subtract 4" from this to determine the maximum length of the dowel

117

rungs. Length depends on the size of your space and the degree of slide incline desired. The following table will help you determine the number of rungs in relation to the overall length and the distance between rungs.

		INCHES BETWEEN RUNGS		
		8"	9"	10"
LENGTH OF THE LADDER IN FEET	3½	5 (5)	3 (5)	6 (4)
	4	4 (6)	6 (5)	4 (5)
	4½	3 (7)	4½ (6)	X
	5	6 (7)	3 (7)	5 (6)
	5½	5 (8)	6 (7)	3 (7)
	6	4 (9)	4½ (8)	6 (7)

The table gives the number of inches from the bottom to measure for the first mark. The number in parentheses is the number of rungs in the ladder. For example, if you were building a 4' ladder with 10" between rungs, the first mark would be at 4" and the next four marks at 14, 24, 34, and 44 inches for a total of five rungs.

• To anchor the ladder to the rungs of a climber, use either a 1×2 across the ends (the same width as the ladder) or rubber bumpers. If the ladder will be used on a carpeted surface, either will do. If it will be used on a wood or linoleum surface, use the anchors and add rubber bumpers to protect the floor.

Construction

1. Cut the 2×3s and dowels to the desired lengths and sand.

2. Measuring from the bottom, mark the points for the rungs according to the table.

3. Drill a 1" diameter hole ½" deep at each mark on both legs of the ladder.

4. Put an ample amount of wood glue in the holes of one leg; insert the dowels and wipe off the excess glue. If the dowels fit snugly (an added benefit), pound them in

with a hammer; use an extra piece of wood between hammer face and dowel to prevent damage to its end.

5. Fill the holes of the other leg with glue. Insert the other end of the dowels to form the ladder. Tap them in, if necessary, as you did before with hammer and wood. Wipe off the excess glue.

6. Lay the ladder on a flat surface to set the glue. Square the ladder (make sure the

rungs are perpendicular to the sides) by using a square, a piece of cardboard, or a book. Squaring the ladder will make the legs sit evenly on the floor and not lean to one side. Use pipe clamps if you have them while the glue sets.

7. Attach the anchors and/or bumpers. Cut two 1×2s the same width as the ladder. Glue and screw them to each end.

8. Sand down or file rough spots, edges, and corners.

9. Polyurethane the wood.

SMALL PLATFORMS

All the climbers can accommodate at least one platform; besides a sitting space, it can be a shelf for dishes, a bed for dolls, or a garage for trucks. Simple plank platforms are described below, but the slides also can double as larger platforms (described later).

The A-frame climbers without a single top rung can accommodate a small platform that is especially handy when a young child wants to climb over and back or just sit up high. This kind of platform and its construction are described under Thomas's Climber.

The box climbers can accommodate two or three platform spaces at different levels or at one level to form a large roof. As many ideas as the adult will have, the children will find ten more ways to pretend and ten more ways to position the planks.

For short spans of 20 inches or less, ½" plywood is acceptable; a piece of pine board or interior grade plywood, at least ¾" thick, is strong enough to hold 60–70 pounds over as much as a 2½-foot span. In order to keep them light and maneuverable, they should be 9–14 inches wide. If you want a large platform space, provide two or three planks side by side.

Materials

- Plywood or pine board forms the platform.
- Four short pieces of 1×2s, about 5" long, anchor a plank to the rungs very securely. Rubber bumpers can also be used.
- Glue and with 1×6 screws secure the 1×2s.

Construction

1. Measure the distance from the outside of one rung on the climber to the outside of the opposite rung; add 3¾″ to determine the length of the plank(s) if you use the 1×2s. If you use the bumpers, add 2″. Too much overhang is dangerous.

2. Lay the plank across the climber; position and mark the places for the 1×2 anchors or bumpers. Allow ½″ extra space between the anchors to allow for variations in widths across rungs.

3. Glue on the 1×2s, screw them into the plank, or do both.

4. Sand and polyurethane the wood.

- Provide experience in gravity, incline, acceleration/deceleration
- Provide experience of height
- Develop sense of orientation in space

SLIDES AND LARGE PLATFORMS

The first plan for a long slide for one child under 35 pounds calls for 3½'–6' lengths of pine board (not particleboard, because it is very brittle). Pictured is a slide made from two 7″ wide boards placed side by side and anchored like the small platforms described previously. There is some flexibility in the boards, and they could crack if used by heavy children.

To increase the weight-bearing load of this kind of slide tremendously, fit the boards over a ladder. The ladder base adds strength yet keeps the slide light enough for children to move it around because it is in two or three pieces. The ladder/slide also has rims to help the children center themselves when sliding down it. Between two climbers or across one large box climber, the same slide becomes an instant platform. To eliminate the seam that you would have when using two thin boards, plywood can also be used for a wider surface.

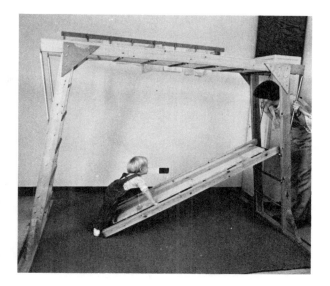
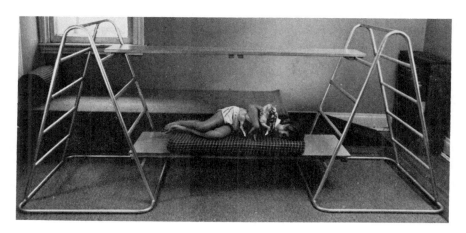

Anchor the slide to the ladder in the same manner as the other platforms, using short lengths of 1×2s. Lay the sliding board over the rungs, centering it. Flip the whole thing over and glue and/or screw on the anchors to the wrong side of the slide on either side of the end rungs.

Another slide/platform without a ladder base is made from interior grade plywood. Plywood can be cut for greater width, and this is an advantage, especially for younger children who do not have great balance or for older children who want to experiment with many different ways to slide. Plywood should not be used without backing over a long span. A large and wide sliding surface can be made with ½" plywood used over the ladder or with 2×2 reinforcement, as in the toddler slide. The toddler slide described under the Toddler Climber is a great rimless surface that can serve a child over a number of years, starting as a toddler climber and then becoming both a slide and a platform on taller climbers.

Another way to increase the strength of ½" plywood and to add rims to a slide is to border it with 1" dowels, handrailing, or 2×2s; size depends on the strength you desire or the extra board that you have left over from another project. The slide pictured is made from ½" plywood, 4' long and 20" wide. The dowels are attached by 1" screws, drilled at 8" intervals from the backside of the slide, and the anchors are two 1×2s. The screw heads and any rough spots on the underside are covered with a bit of glue and felt.

The key to making a good slide, whether the wood used is plywood or pine board, lies in polyurethaning the surface. The more coats, the more slippery the slide. First, sand the wood and edges smooth. Wipe off all sawdust with a slightly damp cloth and dry. Apply one coat of polyurethane and let dry thoroughly. Resand the surface lightly and wipe clean, then apply a second coat. On some woods a third or fourth coat may be necessary to achieve a slick slide, but you should be the judge of how fast you want your children to slide. Also, remember to check the underside, especially the edges, where little fingers grab, for rough wood. Sand and polyurethane this area as well. For large knots or rough spots, cover the surface with glue and felt patches.

12
IMAGINATIVE BOARDS

Imaginative boards will stimulate your child's sense of balance and help him orient himself in the space that surrounds him. The walking boards and the balance board are easy and inexpensive to construct and can be made to suit a child's individual size and skill level. The children can stage circus shows; they will be masters of the pretend tightrope and funny balancing clowns.

- Promote balance
- Develop sense of orientation in space

WALKING BOARDS

Walking boards are such simple pieces of equipment, serving such an obvious developmental skill, that they are often not provided as part of the play environment. Yet children seek out curbs, walls, parking barriers, etc., on which to balance. Walking in a line that places the heel directly in front of the other foot's toes is difficult even for adults.

The younger the child, the wider the walking board should be and the smaller the distance from the ground. For two-year-olds each board is just a little narrower than the child's own stride. As the children get older and their skills improve, the board width can be decreased. To keep up interest and increase the degree of difficulty, supply the child with things to carry, such as a flag, two flags, a paper cup, a half-filled cup of water, a filled cup of water, a tray, a tray with a cup on it, and so on. In the beginning, all the child's energy is centered on the body. Once the child can negotiate the boards with arms flying, he can concentrate on refining the sense of balance and center it closer to the body. Special children, especially those with perceptual handicaps, benefit from practice in balancing.

To add another level of difficulty when the boards have been mastered, glue another 2×4 piece under the base to raise it. Then drill a 2×3 to fit over the dowels for a really skinny beam.

The walking board really need not be a board at all. It can be two chalk lines on a sidewalk, or tape lines on the carpet. If a board *is* used, it can be on the ground or up on bricks, or spanning two climbers. Or you can make the project suggested below. This great beginner project costs about $5 to make.

Materials

- To make this project as it is pictured, cut three 12″ lengths of 2×4.
- Next cut three 4′ lengths of 1×4 or 1×6.
- The third item to be cut are six 1″–1¼″ lengths of 1″ diameter dowels, two for each 2×4.

Construction

1. Drill 1″ diameter holes through the 4′ walking boards.

2. Drill a 1″ hole into the ends of each 2×4 to a ½″ depth; center the drill holes 3″ from the ends.

3. Glue dowels into the bases.

4. Polyurethaning the wood is optional.

5. The walking boards can be placed on the base pieces in many configurations, as shown in the photos.

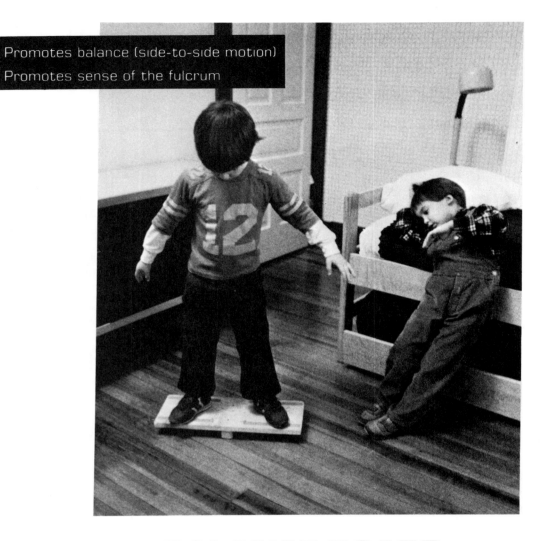

- Promotes balance (side-to-side motion)
- Promotes sense of the fulcrum

BALANCE BOARD

The balance board is a variation of the acrobatic boards on which the jugglers in the circus do their tricks. It is made safer for the preschool set by securing the fulcrum to the board so that it does not fly out from under them. There are three types of boards that cater to different skill levels. To increase the level of difficulty, change the fulcrum from rectangular 1×2 to square 2×2 to round 1½″ dowel (handrailing) as the child becomes more practiced.

The object of this piece of equipment is the stimulation of the sense of balance. In the ears are the semicircular canals, which help humans orient themselves in space; the fluid in these tubes moves with a change in position much like the fluid in a level. The brain translates the information into acceleration/deceleration and position in relation to gravity. (The eyes also help in this work, and that is why, in a tilted funhouse room, one feels "funny"; conflicting information is being processed by the brain.) On the balance board, the child quickly coordinates all this information with the muscles to keep the board parallel to the floor. That is quite a bit of work for a preschooler!

This piece of equipment can be stored easily on a shelf; you might designate a special place to store the large-muscle equipment that is available to the children at any given time so that they always know where to put it away.

Materials

- A piece of plywood or pine board, ¾" thick, about 18" long and 6"–10" wide, forms the top piece. The length and width can vary according to the size of your child and to what is lying around in your wood pile. Do not use particleboard, because it is very brittle.
- To make the wood surface nonskid, add some bathtub no-slip strips.
- Two 1¼" screws secure the fulcrum to the top.
- The easiest fulcrum is a 1×2; for a step up in difficulty, use a 2×2; the most difficult fulcrum for children is a 1½" piece of doweling or handrailing. Cut the fulcrum the same length as the width of the board.

Construction

1. Sand the edges and corners of the wood.
2. Center the fulcrum on the backside of the board and clamp in place.
3. Drill two holes through the top of the board and into the pivot. Screw in the screws until they are flush with the surface. Sand away any rough spots.

4. Add the no-slip surface.
5. To change the fulcrum, remove the screws. Recenter a new fulcrum and clamp. Redrill through the existing holes into the new fulcrum; reinsert the screws.

13
JUMPING EQUIPMENT

Anyone who is over the age of three and is not involved in organized sports probably gives little thought to the skill of jumping. Yet it is a very complex coordination of muscles and mind power.

It's at about age two that children perfect this skill, and doing so requires a lot of work. First, having just learned to walk and run, they have only recently mastered keeping the body balanced while standing and moving. They have also just learned to put one foot in front of the other while keeping one on the ground at any given moment. In a jump, the opposite is demanded: the child must bend at the waist, bringing the chest toward the knees, and then leave the ground with both feet. Then the hands must be coordinated with the upward thrust, and the fear of this strange new motion must be suppressed.

Watch a toddler trying to master this skill for a real treat in both concentration and perseverance! Look particularly at the mistakes made in order to see how the child changes his or her neurological programming from walking to jumping. Now add to the task the different kinds of jumps that children master by age three or four. They jump off and on things, over things, up to things, etc.

Renters who live on upper floors might use the equipment only when the people downstairs are at work. This is also a good outdoor activity.

There are five kinds of jumping motions that the following projects develop in the spirit of fun (not in the spirit of athletic training). They are running and standing high jumps, running and standing broad jumps and the vertical leap. These may sound technical, but they are only sports terms for skills that come naturally to the upright human biped!

All three pieces of jumping equipment, made with 1×2s, cost about $6. What an inexpensive and fun birthday present!

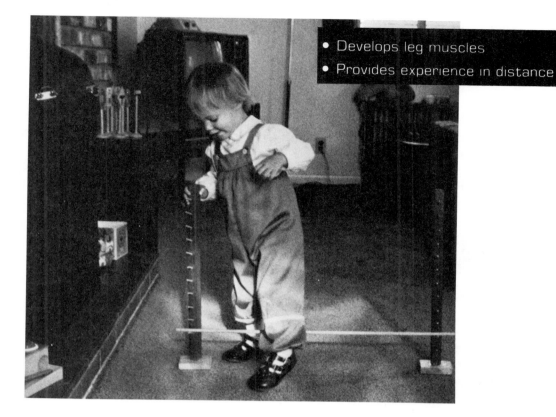

- Develops leg muscles
- Provides experience in distance

RUNNING AND STANDING HIGH JUMP

The high jump is a feat of achieving height (rather than distance) from a still or moving position. Each involves its own fine-tuning of muscles.

The apparatus is basically a 1×2 on a base with lots of pegs to support the crossbar. It can be approached from a running or still start; the jump itself should be done on a rug (not a throw rug). It is lightweight and tippy because it needs to fall over easily if the child does not reach the height. The wood can be left natural in this and all the jumping equipment, and at special intervals or upon making higher achievements the date and child's initials can be written right on the board at the new record spot. It will be a record cherished in months to come.

Materials

- Two 1×2s about 20″ long form the uprights; be careful to cut them squarely so that they stand on the bases without leaning to one side or the other.
- The bases are small pieces of wood. They can be lattice or board, any thickness, large enough to balance the upright and small enough to fall over easily. Pictured are two different kinds of bases on one pair. Each is secured with two 1×6 wood screws and wood glue.
- The pegs are ⅛″ dowel cut in 1¼″ lengths. Total length of dowel depends on the number of pegs; this one has eighteen pegs on each upright for a total of 45 inches of doweling.
- The crossbar is a ¼″ dowel.

Construction

1. Cut all the pieces and sand the wood; also sand the end of each peg where it will stick out.

2. At 1″ or 1½″ intervals (your choice), drill ⅛″ holes at a slight angle, about 20 degrees, to a depth of about ⅜″–½″. Exactness is not necessary.

3. Glue in the pegs and glue the upright onto the base. Prop them carefully at a 90-degree angle in a place where the pair will not be disturbed and let dry.

4. When dry, drill two holes in each base for the screws and drive them in.

5. **Optional:** Write a number next to each peg, starting with one at the bottom, to help a young child match corresponding numbers when setting up the crossbar.

6. Polyurethane the wood.

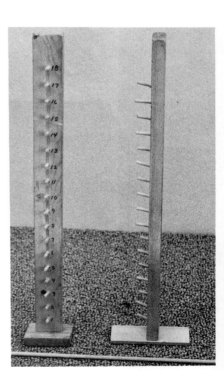

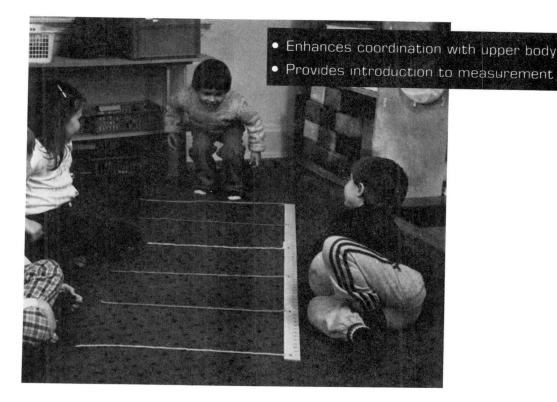

- Enhances coordination with upper body
- Provides introduction to measurement

RUNNING AND STANDING BROAD JUMP

Children broad jump over the sidewalk, from rug to rug, and over their siblings or sleeping pet. Providing this apparatus does not necessarily mean that they will give up that form of recreation entirely, but it is a safer outlet. There are two ideas presented to channel this kind of energy.

The first is sewing a measuring tape down the side of a long exercise mat like Buse's mat described in Chapter 9. The child can measure and compare distances on successive jumps.

The other project to mark the length of a jump is made with a piece of lattice or a yardstick and 24-inch pieces of colored yarn. The older the child, the longer the measurer needs to be. (Test your children before you start constructing to see how far they can jump. If you underestimate, the equipment will become obsolete. The foul line is two colors of yarn twisted together and knotted every 6 inches for a more visible start. Successive strings are singular and in different colors. To put it away, the child rolls it up and stores it behind the bookcase. This is a great project for five-year-olds to make all by themselves if you have a hand drill.

Materials

- Use a yardstick or 4'–6' of 1×2 or lattice to form the board. Lattice is a presanded and knot-free baseboard wood that comes in 1¼" or 1¾" width; either is usable.
- Use six or seven 2' strips of narrow ribbon or yarn.

RINGS, SWINGS & CLIMBING THINGS

Construction

1. Draw on the wood your own inch marks or use a 4′ hardware store "yardstick." Drill small holes through the wood at each foot mark.

2. Tie the colored yarn through the holes with a knot at the end to keep it from fraying.

134

Stimulates eye/foot and eye/hand coordination

VERTICAL LEAPER

With this piece of equipment, the child is trying to jump and reach as high as the legs can push. It does not have *boy* or *girl* written on it, so do not discriminate against the females and deny them this kind of physical expression.

Leaping and jumping are skills that improve with practice. Besides helping them develop a specific skill, you are offering the children a chance to master to a high degree the muscles of their body. The procedure the children should follow is to repeat the jump three times in a row, keeping their eye on the bell.

The vertical leaper is fun and easy to make. It is actually a larger version of the high jump; the same drilling technique is employed. For a one-child family, 15 inches of 1×2 will give the child plenty of room to grow. For a multisibling family, the 1×2 will need to be 2½–3 feet long to accommodate a variety of heights.

Materials

- The board is a 1×2 about 15"–36" long.
- A ⅜" dowel about 9" long holds the bell.
- The spring should be 2"–3" long so that the child does not have a shot at hitting the immovable dowel, only the bell.
- The bell pictured is an oversized jingle bell; a cowbell or any other bell is also appropriate.

Construction

1. Sand the rough surfaces and corners and then mark the 1×2 at 1″ or 1½″ intervals for the drill holes.

2. Drill ⅜″ holes almost all the way through the 1×2 at a slight angle (about 20–30 degrees) so that the dowel will slant upward in its slot. Exactness is not necessary.

3. Secure the spring by slipping the loop over the dowel; pinch it with pliers if necessary for a tight fit. Attach the bell to the opposite end and pinch the end of the spring closed over the bell.

4. Attach to a wall, a door frame, or the back of a door with two screws. For renters, it could be clamped with small C-clamps to a door.

14
WHEEL TOYS

Pushing and pulling! These are two activities that children love as much for their own sake as for carting around toys and each other. The whole body—arms, shoulder, back, and legs—is involved. And these wheel toys can be used indoors and out.

For the toddler, the lesson of transferred material ties in closely with object constancy; an object here or there is still the same object regardless of the change in its environment. For preschool children, the value in transferring material lies in the power they feel in moving things about in space. The pretend value of the belly board and cart is also part of their advantages.

• Stimulates alternating left/right movement (in crawling)

BELLY BOARD

The belly board has two different actions; the first is self-propelled, and the second is propelled by someone else. The self-propelled motion shares the rhythm of crawling and is excellent stimulation for the movement of alternating left-right-left (and a well-developed sense of this movement has been associated with better reading skills). The child lying on the board on his or her belly uses arms and legs to crawl around the floor.

As a pull toy, the belly board is a transport for siblings, friends, dolls, blocks, sticks, etc. The handles give a rider stability without having to wrap fingers around the rope or the edge of the board.

Children from age two on will enjoy the belly board. **One caution:** When pulled by a *tall* person using a short rope, the belly board will tend to dump backward.

Materials

- Use a plywood base, 18″ × 18″ × ¾″. The seat is as long as it is wide for stability when being pulled.
- The front wheels are swivels, while the back two are on fixed axles. They cost $1.50–$8.00 apiece; generally, the better the wheel (more heavy-duty, better ball bearings, rubber instead of plastic wheels), the less noise it will make on a sidewalk or hard surface floor. Spend the greater amount if parent, child, or neighborhood is sensitive to noise. Do not buy small plastic furniture coasters; they make a tremendous racket and tend to crack.
- Two brass or aluminum handles are fine.
- A 4′–5′ length of nylon rope is needed for the pull.

- If the wheels and handles are not sold with screws, ask the hardware person for ¾" screws that fit the holes in their bases.
- Padding or carpeting is optional. Sand and polyurethane the wood to seal it if it is not covered.

Construction

1. If you are not covering the wood, sand and polyurethane it first.

2. Mark the holes for wheels and handles. Drill the appropriate-diameter holes into the wood the length of the screws. Drill a ½" diameter hole through the wood where the rope pull will be tied.

3. Attach each wheel and turn the screws just until tight. If the screws are overtightened, the threads will strip the wood.

4. If the wood is to be covered, cut a piece of carpeting and tack it on, cutting out the space for the handles and the pulling rope.

5. Tie on the rope handle and put a loop in the pulling end.

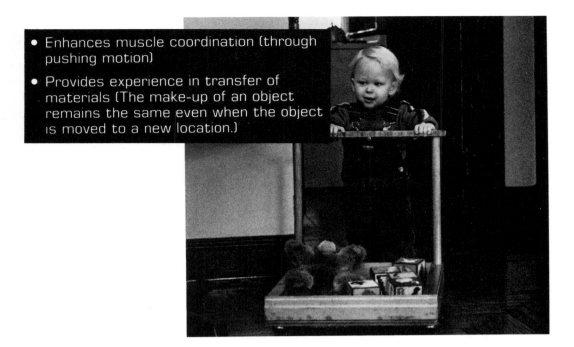

- Enhances muscle coordination (through pushing motion)

- Provides experience in transfer of materials (The make-up of an object remains the same even when the object is moved to a new location.)

PUSHCART

The pushcart is an ideal first walker for young toddlers; it is stable and weighty enough not to tip or run away from them. For older children it becomes the grocery cart, wheelbarrow, block holder, or taxicab. Indoors, with a bumper, or outside on the sidewalk, the pushcart provides children with a means of moving their environment.

It is deceptively easy to make and it costs about $6 for the wood. The cost of the wheels, as for the belly board, depends on the quality.

Materials

- The base is a piece of plywood ¾" thick and cut 18" × 18". Remember, some lumberyards can cut wood to order.
- The right and left sides are 2×3s cut 16½" long. The front panels are as wide as the base (18"), as tall as the 2×3 (2½"—remember, 2×3s are actually smaller than 2" × 3"), and ¾" thick. Pictured is a piece of woodwork molding, but a 1 × 3 (really ¾" × 2½") is adequate.
- Two 16"–18" lengths of 1" diameter dowel are needed. For toddler use, cut the shorter length.
- The handle is a 1×2, 19" long.
- The two swivels and the two set wheels are the same kind called for in the belly board directions.
- Six 1½×6 and ten 1¼×6 wood screws secure the sides. You also need sixteen ¾" screws to attach the wheels. Ask the hardware person to fit them to the holes in the wheel bases.
- A bumper is a good idea for indoor use. Cut a 1×2 that is 1½" wider than the cart and wrap it with carpet. Use two 2" screws or nails to attach it to the front of the finished cart. A number of rubber bumpers, sold at hardware stores, can also be screwed into the cart at the corners and across the front. One last idea is to tack on 10 inches of old hose or 1" plastic tubing around each corner as a bumper.

Construction

1. Cut all wood and sand the edges.

2. If extra time is available, glue the 2×3s to the base and let set; it makes drilling much easier. Otherwise, position the 2×3s, clamp, and turn over. Drill through the bottom of the base into the sides as deep as the screws will be going. Next tighten in the 1½″ screws. Glue will help lubricate the threads.

3. Attach the front panels to the 2×3s by gluing them in place, drilling two holes on each side, and then turning in the screws.

4. Next drill 1″ diameter holes for the dowels into the 2×3s, ¾″ deep and 2″ from the end.

5. Drill 1″ diameter holes into the 1×2 handle about ½″ deep, matching it to the distance between the dowels in the base.

6. Attach the wheels as outlined in the belly board directions—swivels on the front and fixed-axle wheels on the back.

7. Glue the dowels into the 2×3s and into the handle. Put a 1″ screw down through the handle into the dowels.

8. Polyurethane the wood.

15
LET'S PRETEND

In this chapter is a selection of miscellaneous toys that both encourage large-muscle work and spark children's imaginations for games of "let's pretend. . . ." What could be more desirable for the children (and you) than easy-to-make equipment that keeps your children moving and engrossed in the fantasies that they can make "real" with colorful streamers, custom-designed hobbyhorses, and a big pile of large, soft building blocks? The ring toss project in this chapter also introduces young children to counting and to the fun of an organized game that can still be noncompetitive.

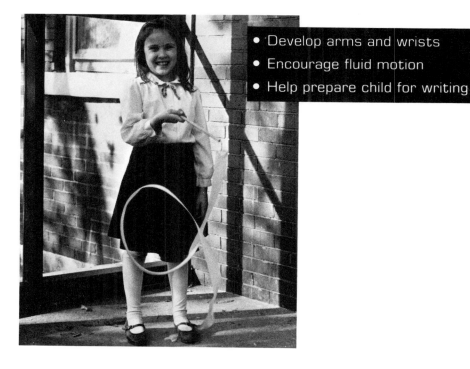

- Develop arms and wrists
- Encourage fluid motion
- Help prepare child for writing

STREAMERS

Children of all ages love a streamer. It provides a large-muscle activity for the arm that is as beautiful as it is fun. Children can draw a circle, write a name, or lasso an imaginary horse without knocking over a lamp (at least the ribbon won't).

The length of the streamer depends on the length of the child; add about one foot to the child's height for ribbon length. A ribbon that is too long will get tangled around the child and will not inspire success. Even a toddler enjoys a streamer; a ribbon about 18" long is negotiable for the younger ones. A beautiful variation is to use two colors of ribbon in one streamer for a double-tailed effect. Add some music for very creative movement!

To store the streamer, keep it in a small box or on a tray on the toy shelf. You might have noticed that toy boxes are never mentioned in this book. Toy boxes are a conglomeration of toys; they are catchalls, garbage cans, disorganized messes. If toys are to be respected, they need the integrity of being stored carefully and in a pleasing visual manner. Can you visualize the streamer at the bottom of the toy box wrapped around a truck? Now visualize it in a box as one of eight or nine toys stored on a low shelf. Which streamer is going to last and be used more often? Which truck, too?

Materials

- The handle is a ⅜" dowel about 10" long.
- The streamer is satin ribbon about 1½" wide that has a *selvaged edge;* that means that the edge cannot unravel. (Some inexpensive package-wrapping ribbon is cut in strips from large sheets, and the edges are not sealed.)
- To connect dowel and ribbon, you need eyelet, fishing swivel with clip, and a paper clip.

Construction

1. Hammer a starter hole for the eyelet in the end of the dowel with a very small nail. Insert the eyelet.

2. Fold over about ½" of the ribbon and cut a very small hole in the fold. Put the end of the swivel through the hole and attach the paper clip to the swivel. Sew the paperclip into the ribbon fold with a few stitches. Hem the other end of the ribbon.

3. Attach the clip end of the swivel to the eyelet. Voilà!

- Develops wrist movement
- Enhances eye/hand coordination
- Involves timing (through throwing motion)
- Encourages game playing
- Develops "your turn, my turn" social skills
- Promotes sense of quantity

RING TOSS

This is a great starting project for any adult and also for a child who wants to be involved in Mom's or Dad's work. The skills necessary to make the ring toss are the same for many of the wood projects, including the climbers, but on a smaller scale. Use up the wood in the lumber pile (yours or your friendly neighborhood lumberyard's), and then the cost of the ring toss will be the cost of the dowel, about 50¢.

Ring toss for two- or three-year-olds is more like a game of ring drop; they stand directly over the pegs. This is a logical thing to do (if you think like a two- or three-year-old) because they are assuring themselves of success. Why should they set themselves up for failure by standing four or five feet away? As children get more skilled at coordinating aim, release, and the velocity of the throw, they will naturally test themselves, although still within a range that is likely to assure success.

This game can be played alone or with a group. If you are concerned about avoiding competition, encourage the family to play toward a total point goal. For example, play for ten ringers, no matter who gets them; thus the whole family wins. When the goal is success (which children naturally set for themselves) and not failure (which adults usually set in the form of challenge), children build a self-image of "I can do it."

Ring toss can be an addition and memory game as well as a large-muscle exercise. During the first year, simply add one number for each successful toss. Then, the following year, each of the five different pegs can be assigned a different number, and each score can be added to the previous number of points made.

Note: Step-by-step illustrations accompany the ring toss project in Chapter 5, "A Project for the Novice Carpenter."

Materials

- The base piece of wood or plywood is at least 6″ × 10″ and as large as 12″ × 16″.
- The dowels should be ¼″–¾″ in diameter. Cut 3–9 pegs, depending on the size of the base and your preference, each about 4″ long.
- Rings can be plastic bracelets, mason jar gaskets, or rings cut from an inner tube. They also can be made from the same rope as the doorway gym. Cut a length 12″ long and thread a bead over the rope; generously glue the ends together. Slide the bead over the seam and let dry.

Construction

1. Sand all wood, slightly rounding the corners of the base and the top of the pegs.

2. Mark the pattern for the pegs (one in each corner and one in the center) and drill through the board with the same-size drill bit as the dowel's diameter:

3. Put glue in the holes and insert the pegs. Wipe off the excess glue and let dry. Cover the back with felt for a protective surface.

4. **Optional:** Write a number at the base of each peg for the values of the ringer with water-base marker and polyurethane.

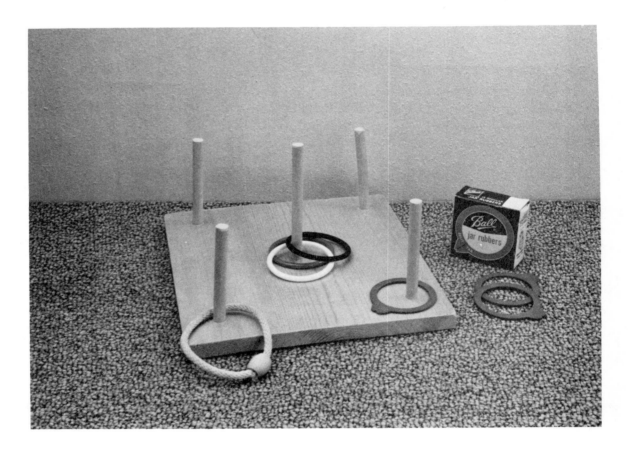

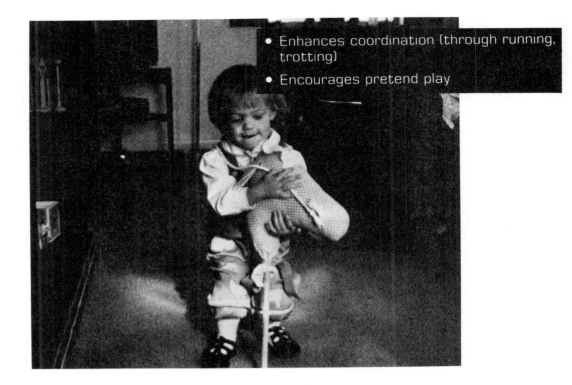

- Enhances coordination (through running, trotting)
- Encourages pretend play

HOBBYHORSE

A hobbyhorse is a traditional toy that can have a very personal touch. Adult or child can design it in any color or style. It doesn't even have to be a horse; it can be a unicorn, an elephant, a mouse, or a favorite mascot. Children from 18 months on will enjoy pretending their favorite fantasy.

The special feature of this hobbyhorse, besides its individual custom design, is that the stick is proportioned especially for the child and for use indoors. It is short enough, only 20"–22" long, so that when the child turns, it does not knock over and into all that is in the room. This small change in what is otherwise a standard toy makes it a very safe and successful plaything.

A large, adult-sized sock forms the head of the animal and is stuffed with store-bought stuffing, old clothes with the buttons and zippers cut out, fabric scraps, etc. If you want a slightly different kind of head, a pattern can be drawn on two pieces of material. It should be a slighty inflated design because, when it is stuffed, it takes on smaller dimensions. If the design is a large one like the elephant pictured, Styrofoam packing material can be added to the cloth stuffing to keep the head lighter in weight.

Because all these materials are usually found around the house, the cost of the hobbyhorse is the cost of the dowel.

Materials

- The head is either a sock or a design of your own making.
- The dowel is 20"–22" long; it can be ⅜"–1" in diameter.
- A few thumb or upholstery tacks secure the head to the stick.
- Assorted decorations.

Construction

1. Find a sock or draw a design on the wrong side of two pieces of fabric. With right sides of the two pieces together, cut out the design. Sew together, leaving open the place where the stick will be inserted. Turn the head right side out.

2. Stuff the front half of the head until it is stiff.

3. Cut the dowel and wrap the end in material like a cotton swab to provide a cushion for the end of the stick.

4. Insert the dowel into the head and stuff around the stick, leaving about 2" unstuffed at the opening.

5. Hammer in two or three thumb or upholstery tacks through the sock or fabric at the end of the stuffing to secure the head to the stick. Cover the tacks by wrapping a wide ribbon around the cuff and knot tightly.

6. Decorate with felt, lace, buttons, yarn, jewels. Add reins (made of rope or other material) or whatever grabs your fancy. If this is a present for a young child or a very oral child who might attempt to chew on small buttons and the like, use only felt and yarn to prevent injury to the child.

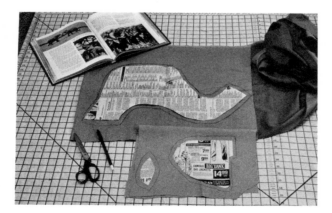

- Stimulate eye/hand coordination (through stacking)
- Promote sense of concepts and mathematical ratios
- Encourage pretend play

SOFT BLOCKS

This piece of equipment has the longest service life of any project in the book. Beginning at age 1, children delight in carrying and stacking the blocks. At 2, they make roads to walk on and barriers to mark their houses. At 3, they make stacks to knock down. When they are 4, the children have great mock battles and bopping matches to test their aggressive skills. At 5, they build beautifully elaborate buildings with entrances and windows. At 6, they build furniture, beds, and doll cribs, cars, and boats. Between 7 and 10 they repeat all these activities.

At 21 or 35, guess who also likes to build houses and bop a child or two? Block building has its own developmental skill levels; do not be disappointed if your 3- or 4-year-old does not build Taj Mahals like you do. They will do so when they are 5 or 6.

The soft blocks are made of urethane foam and are covered with a thin (and colorful) cotton. If one is hopelessly soiled, it can be thrown in the washer and then *air*-dried, (not tumble-dried), but the blocks do not get very dirty with indoor use. They are so light and yet stackable that they are very safe toys for building tall towers and for young children to toss around.

The one problem that you might have with the soft blocks is their storage. First, they need a large space to be stacked; their bulk increases greatly if they're just heaped in a toy box. The blocks should have a permanent spot near an open building space to encourage the children to put them away. This sometimes can be the second problem. Since there are several of them, the children often feel that it is a lot of work to put them away. The older the child, the less the burden of a large quantity. Five or six blocks are appropriate for a one-year-old; a two-year-old can handle ten. It might be necessary for you to put them away, out of sight for a few days, when the children are not being responsible for them. Once they get the idea that a rule, putting the soft blocks away, is an unbreakable one, they will realize that they have the choice of picking up after themselves or of not having the blocks to play with. The key to the success of this self-responsibility approach is the adult's commitment to the time and energy needed to establish the precedent.

Twenty to twenty-five soft blocks are sufficient for major construction and still few enough to put away. The ones pictured are carved from blocks of foam 4 inches thick. The standard width sold in most stores is 22 inches, and the first diagram shows a layout for three different sizes of blocks with no wasted foam. The number you make in each size is your decision.

Another possibility, although there will be some waste, is to cut them according to the second diagram. (Use the scraps to stuff a hobbyhorse or punching bag.) The benefit is that the blocks have a ratio for relationships in their dimensions. It is 4:6:12 (or 1:1.5:3). The child, in stacking them, comes to know unconsciously that one of this block equals two of that block or three of the other blocks. This is called *sensorimotor knowledge* because it is knowing through the senses and the action of the muscles and not through conscious reasoning. The soft blocks allow great premath work, teaching quantity and ratio.

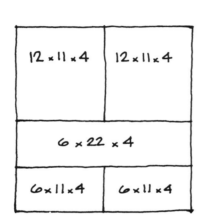

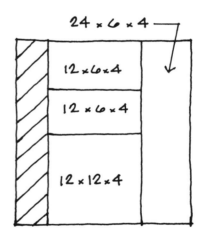

Materials

- Urethane foam blocks 4" thick are normally sold in 22" widths and in 24", 48", and 76" lengths. One 4" × 22" × 24" block yields eight small blocks.
- Light cotton/polyester fabric in one or a variety of colors. For 36" wide material, two small blocks can be covered with ⅔ yard. For 48" wide material, two small blocks take ½ yard.

Construction

1. Mark the pattern for cutting the foam on its surface with a dark marker, being careful to draw straight lines. It is important to measure accurately in order to make blocks that stack squarely.

2. Mark the same pattern on the reverse side so that, when you carve up the block, you have guidelines to help you stay perpendicular to the surface.

3. *This is a messy step, so do it outside or in an otherwise cleanable environment.* With a long and sharp serrated knife, like a bread knife, saw along the lines that you drew. It would be helpful to have someone on the other side of the foam to steady it and watch the knife for deviations from your lines.

4. Cut the appropriate size of material and wrap a block as if it were a present. Fold under the long seam about ½"; whip-stitch all seams closed with doubled thread. (This step takes a bit of time to complete, multiplied by twenty or twenty-five blocks, so plan on a few nights of sewing in front of the TV.)

5. Find a place in your play area to store the blocks.

16
MOVING THE INDOOR EQUIPMENT OUTSIDE

It might be hard to get out of the rut of thinking that some activities are outdoor sports while others belong indoors. Now that you are out of that rut, with the doorway gym, climbers, and other equipment as indoor activities, it's time to take them back outdoors. With one set of equipment (and one investment), the spaces can be interchangeable. If you have a yard or porch, include that space in your overall plans for child-oriented places.

THE DOORWAY GYM OUTSIDE

There are many places to set up the doorway gym outside. An old swing set frame can be rejuvenated with new equipment. Another great spot is on large porches; if the ceiling is high, hang a length of chain and S-hooks to reachable height, accommodating the indoor gym pieces. A third outdoor spot is under a second-floor wood deck; it is a ready-built frame. Survey the spot for safety; the older the child, the larger the arc the swing will make.

There is usually less supervision in an outdoor space, so you will have to be extra careful that the child can work safely and independently. The exercise mat can even be brought out to cushion a porch surface.

The doorway gym equipment can be left permanently outdoors with some changes. For the soft swing, make the seat out of a canvas suitable for porch furniture. The aluminum trapeze, plastic rings, and tetherball can remain outside

153

in the rain, as can the knotted rope, if it does not include the wooden beads. The rope ladder and baby swing are not suited for continuous outdoor exposure as the wood is not pressure-treated. The punching bag is not a good piece of equipment to leave outside permanently either. These must be brought inside each night.

MOVING THE CLIMBERS AND OTHER EQUIPMENT OUTDOORS

The polyurethaned climbers or other wood equipment should not be left outdoors in wet weather. Being climbed on after the child gets out of the wading pool will not harm them, but a night in rain or snow will weaken the wood. If you have outdoor space and intend to use it often, build a highly portable A-frame climber, taking it outdoors during the day and storing it indoors at night. If you have a *large* outdoor space, build two A-frames and lots of accessories for highly creative equipment.

Whether setting up the outdoor space or the indoor space, remember that *all* of the jumping, riding, throwing things, etc., do not have to be available at one time. Store some away and then switch the stored and the used pieces in mid-season for a fresh environment!

INDEX